Go Figure!
Exploring Figurative Language

Timothy Rasinski, Ph.D.
Jerry Zutell, Ph.D.
Melissa Cheesman Smith, M.Ed.

Publishing Credits

Corinne Burton, M.A.Ed., *President;* Conni Medina, M.A.Ed., *Managing Editor ;* Emily Smith, M.A.Ed., *Content Director;* Angela Johnson-Rogers, M.F.A., M.S.Ed., *Editor;* Lee Aucoin, *Senior Graphic Designer;* Kevin Pham, *Graphic Designer;* Kyleena Harper, *Assistant Editor*

Image Credits

All images from iStock and Shutterstock.

Standards

Shell Education

A division of Teacher Created Materials
5301 Oceanus Drive
Huntington Beach, CA 92649-1030

http://www.tcmpub.com/shell-education

ISBN 978-1-4258-1626-1

©2017 Shell Education Publishing, Inc.

Table of Contents

Introduction and Research

Figurative language is embedded in both written and oral language across all content areas. Familiarizing students with common figures of speech enables them to better understand the world around them in their reading and their social encounters. Figures of speech are a fun way to engage students with phrases in your classroom through bulletin boards, interactive activities, and social speech opportunities.

The overarching term *figurative language* encompasses words or phrases that mean something more or different from their literal definitions. Figurative language includes words used in nonliteral ways through different figures of speech for the purposes of enhancing language and making it livelier. There are many types of figures of speech in the English language, including idioms, proverbs, similes, metaphors, personification, hyperbole, and oxymorons. (See page 7 for more information on the types of figures of speech.) Inferred meaning of a figurative phrase is not something that students learn by dissecting the individual words. Rather, students must study and understand the context of the words or phrases through reading, social speech, and cultural experiences.

"Literal" vs. "Figurative"

Figurative meanings are often quite different from the literal meanings. The *literal* meaning of a figure of speech means exactly what each word says. The *figurative* meaning of a figure of speech *implies* or *infers* what the phrase together says in a different way, more than the surface or literal meaning.

This series was designed to make this important part of word study interactive and relevant for students. So, when it comes to teaching vocabulary, don't *sit on the fence*, don't *have cold feet*, and don't *try to pull any strings*. Let us do the honors and *make heads or tails* out of teaching figurative language for your students. Before you know it, you'll be *standing on your own two feet* and teaching figurative language will be *as comfortable as an old shoe*. Moreover, your students will *fall head over heels* in love with figurative language as they read and write.

Content-Area Themes

When teachers merge literacy into content-area learning, students' vocabularies are improved in positive ways. While figures of speech are not meant to directly teach content, the meanings of the words relate to the content the students are learning and allow students to see how words can play on each other, often through multiple meanings.

Effective teachers can connect literacy to the content areas, which makes for authentic practice and learning. By studying figurative language, and specifically idioms and proverbs, within the content areas, students can associate these figures of speech to academic vocabulary and words they hear in science, social studies, and mathematics. This book is divided into content-area themes so students can connect learning about these idioms and proverbs to content-area vocabulary.

Introduction and Research (cont.)

Why Is Figurative Language Important?

Figurative language is part and parcel of oral and written language. Use of figures of speech goes back thousands of years and allows writing to come alive in creative and engaging ways. English is rich in idioms (Harris and Hodges 1995), an important type of figurative language. Since English is filled with such language, it can be a challenge to understand (Blachowicz and Fisher 2014). This is especially true for English language learners who have had even less exposure to experiences involving the figurative meanings of phrases in the English language.

Every learner comes across figurative language that can be difficult to understand because they have not been previously exposed to the figures of speech and/or were not told the meanings or given sufficient clues to make sense of the figurative implications of the words. Children, by their very nature of having limited life experiences, are more likely to encounter figurative language they do not understand. Struggling readers have special difficulty with figurative language because they lack textual experience with it and because their focus tends to be on unlocking the pronunciations of individual words and accessing their literal meanings. English language learners have special difficulty with figurative language because of a lack of English experience and because idioms rarely translate directly from one language to another. Therefore, teachers need to spend time explicitly teaching figurative language in the classroom.

The use of figurative language in writing is a characteristic of high-quality literature (Blachowicz and Fisher 2014). Authors include idioms and proverbs in their writing to clarify their messages and make the writing more interesting to readers. Blachowicz and Fisher (2014) argue that authors use figurative language, including unusual juxtapositions of words, to draw attention to and enlighten us about various aspects of our world. However, if a reader is unfamiliar with the figurative phrase in the text, then he or she is likely to have a poor or limited understanding of those aspects.

Research indicates that children understand relatively simple figures of speech in familiar contexts (e.g., similes and metaphors). As text increases in difficulty, the figures of speech being used become less familiar and more complex. Thus, figurative language can contribute to difficulty in comprehension of rigorous texts. This book focuses on some of those items less familiar to children, especially in the form of idioms and proverbs.

The Importance of Figurative Language

- Figurative language saturates the English language.

- Figurative language has a major impact on written and oral comprehension.

- Figurative language adds a richness, color, and creativity to reading, writing, and thinking.

Introduction and Research (cont.)

The Importance of Studying Figures of Speech

The National Reading Panel (2000) has identified vocabulary as an essential component of effective literacy instruction. When students do not know the meanings of the words and phrases in the texts they read, they are likely to experience difficulty in sufficiently understanding those same texts. Some of the most difficult sentences to understand contain words and phrases that are not meant to express their literal meanings but their figurative ones.

Figures of speech are found everywhere. Students need to be exposed to many different figures of speech for general cultural awareness and to develop an understanding that not all words and expressions are meant to be taken literally. Thus, the study of figurative language is certainly worthwhile, as great awareness and understanding of such language structures can enhance students' understanding of the texts they read. Despite the fact that today's college and career readiness standards recognize the importance of studying figurative language, most core reading or language arts curricular programs do not provide adequate instructional coverage of figurative language. Therefore, the *Go Figure! Exploring Figurative Language* series provides specific and engaging instruction on figurative language for students. As students become more acquainted with figurative language, reading comprehension and written composition will improve.

The major intent of this series is to improve students' reading comprehension and overall reading achievement. However, as noted earlier, high-quality writing is marked by the use of figurative language. Thus, improving students' writing skills is very likely to be a secondary benefit of using *Go Figure! Exploring Figurative Language*. As students' knowledge and use of figurative language improves and expands, the quality of their writing will likely show measurable gains as well.

Steps to Introduce Figures of Speech

1. Read the figure of speech.
2. Think about the literal meaning of the phrase.
3. Predict the figurative meaning of the phrase.
4. Use resources to discover the meaning of the figure of speech.
5. Read the figure of speech in context, as it might be used in the text.
6. Talk about why an author might choose this figure of speech and how it would affect the overall meaning of the text.

Introduction and Research (cont.)

Definitions of Selected Figures of Speech

It's easy to confuse the various types of figurative language. Although all these types of figures of speech are not used in the book, this chart serves as a good reference for you and your students.

	Definition	Example
allusion	referring to a person, place, or thing without mentioning it directly	She acted like a *Scrooge*.
euphemism	the substitution of a mild or pleasant word for one considered offensive	The family dog *passed away*.
hyperbole	an exaggerated statement	I'm so hungry *I could eat a horse*!
idiom	a phrase that means something very different from the literal meaning	He was *as hungry as a bear*.
irony	a statement or situation that is the opposite of what you expect	That's as strange as *a pilot with a fear of heights*.
metaphor	a direct comparison between two unlike things	The *moon is a mirror*.
oxymoron	contradictory terms that appear side by side	The guilty pet sat in *deafening silence* as her owner cleaned up the kitchen.
paradox	a statement that appears to contradict itself	The story was *bittersweet*.
personification	an inanimate object is given human qualities	*The angry sea seethed endlessly.*
proverb	a memorable saying based on facts and generally thought to be true	*Do unto others as you want done unto you.*
pun	a play on words	Fish are *smart* because they live in *schools*.
simile	a comparison (usually formed with "like" or "as") between two things	Her eyes were *as bright as the sun*.

How to Use This Series

Activity Descriptions

Teacher Overview Page

Purpose: This page provides organization for each unit. On this page you will find the following:

1. The five figurative phrases used in the unit
2. Additional figures of speech for the theme
3. Answers for each lesson in the unit
4. Overview materials needed for the lessons in the unit

Match That Figure!

Purpose: Provide definitions and orient students to the meaning of each figure of speech.

Preparation: Copy this page with nothing on the back, as it will be cut at the bottom.

Procedure

1. Have students cut apart the definitions at the bottom of the page.
2. Explain each figure of speech while students glue each card next to its corresponding figure of speech. Or, allow students to match the definitions with the figures of speech first and then discuss them.
3. Tell students to draw pictures to help them remember the figurative meanings of the figures of speech.
4. This sheet is great for students to reference while completing the other activities.

Would You Rather?

Purpose: Allow students to practice using the figures of speech in context.

Preparation: Copy the activity page and distribute to students.

Procedure

1. Have students read each sentence provided and choose the figure of speech that best completes each sentence.
2. At the end, have students create their own sentences using the figure of speech not used in one of the previous sentences. (If a student chooses an incorrect figure of speech in a previous sentence and then writes a sentence with the wrong figure of speech, he or she should still be given credit for the correct sentence.)

How to Use This Series (cont.)

Activity Descriptions (cont.)

Meaningful Words

Purpose: Provide exploration of multiple meanings of words in context. **Note:** Sometimes, the words will have very close meanings but are different parts of speech. For example, students may have to choose between "doctor" as a person or an action. This helps students pay attention to detail and use familiar words in new ways.

Preparation: Copy the activity page or display it for the class to view.

Procedure

1. For each activity set, have students read the chosen word and review the different meanings of the word. **Note:** Specific definitions were chosen for each word but not every common definition was used.

2. Have students choose which definition matches how the word is used in the context of each sentence. Students can underline or highlight which words they used as context clues to aid in choosing a definition.

3. For the challenge activity, students choose one definition and write a sentence that correctly shows context for the meaning of the word with the chosen definition.

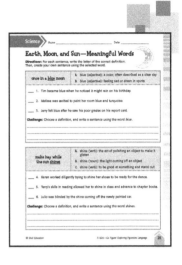

Wacky Writing

Purpose: Practice the meanings of the figures of speech through application in writing.

Preparation: Copy the activity page or display it for the class to view.

Procedure

1. Have students read and answer each prompt.
2. Answers will vary, and correct completion is based on correct application of the figure of speech in the answer.

How to Use This Series (cont.)

Activity Descriptions (cont.)

Say What? Extensions

Purpose: Apply knowledge of the figures of speech through critical thinking, language practice, and creativity during challenging and fun activities.

Preparation: Read each activity ahead of time to determine what supplies the students may need, and have these supplies available to the students (e.g., flashcards, markers).

Procedure

1. Have students select and complete two of the three activities provided. Some activities are completed individually, while others are completed with partners or in small groups.
2. **Optional:** You may decide to have students choose only one activity, or complete all activities if time permits.

Correlation to the Standards

Shell Education is committed to producing educational materials that are research and standards based. As part of this effort, we have correlated all of our products to the academic standards of all 50 states, the District of Columbia, the Department of Defense Dependents Schools, and all Canadian provinces.

Purpose and Intent of Standards

The Every Student Succeeds Act (ESSA) mandates that all states adopt challenging academic standards that help students meet the goal of college and career readiness. While many states already adopted academic standards prior to ESSA, the act continues to hold states accountable for detailed and comprehensive standards. Standards are statements that describe the criteria necessary for students to meet specific academic goals. They define the knowledge, skills, and content students should acquire at each level. State standards are used in the development of our products, so educators can be assured they meet state academic requirements.

How to Find Standards Correlations

To print a customized correlation report of this product for your state, visit our website at **www.teachercreatedmaterials.com/administrators/correlations/** and follow the online directions. If you require assistance in printing correlation reports, please contact our Customer Service Department at 1-877-777-3450.

How to Use This Series (cont.)

Extension Activities Descriptions

Each extension activity focuses on one type of learning: visual, kinesthetic, auditory, linguistic, spatial, intrapersonal, or interpersonal. This chart explains each extension activity in this book.

Extension	Type of Learning	Explanation
Actor's Studio	kinesthetic	Act out each figure of speech using body motions for a peer to guess.
Comic Strip	visual	Create a comic strip to demonstrate the humor of misunderstanding a figure of speech and how that can lead to confusion.
Conversation Starter	linguistic, interpersonal	Write a dialogue to practice applying the meaning of each figure of speech.
Example and Non-example	linguistic	To gain a better understanding of the meanings, think, write, and discuss examples and non-examples of figures of speech.
The Extra Mile	interpersonal, kinesthetic	Use the phrase *to go the extra mile* in everyday situations.
Figurative and Literal	kinesthetic	Using creativity, draw literal and figurative interpretations of figures of speech.
Friendly Letter	interpersonal	Write a friendly letter using the term *solid as a rock*.
Matching Game	kinesthetic	Practice matching each definition to its corresponding phrase in a fun and engaging way.
Memory Game	kinesthetic	Test memory and understanding of the figures of speech by using index cards to paraphrase the definitions.
Mime Time	kinesthetic	Use body language and gestures to show comprehension of figures of speech.
No Man Is an Island	intrapersonal	Use the phrase *no man is an island* to complete a creative writing activity.
Poetry Time	musical, linguistic	Create a rhyming poem, verse, or song to define each figure of speech.
Read All About It	auditory, linguistic	Write a creative short story for a newspaper using at least two figures of speech.
Say It, Don't Spray It!	linguistic	Write a short story using all the figures of speech.
Short Story	linguistic	Use at least two figures of speech to write a personal story.
Tell Me a Tale	linguistic	Construct a fairy tale using multiple figures of speech.
Tunnel Vision	kinesthetic, intrapersonal	Apply the phrase *light at the end of the tunnel* to a personal goal.
Word Association	linguistic	Associate one or two words with each figure of speech.
Valentine's Day Card	linguistic, interpersonal	Use a figure of speech to construct a Valentine's Day card for a historical couple.

Figures of Speech

» follow to the ends of the earth   » once in a blue moon

» go to bed with the sun   » over the moon

» make hay while the sun shines

Overview

Students will enjoy learning about Earth-, Moon- and Sun-related figures of speech through the activities in this section. For detailed instructions on how to implement the activities in this lesson, see pages 8–10.

Materials

> copies of *Earth, Moon, and Sun—Match That Figure!* (page 13)

> copies of *Earth, Moon, and Sun—Would You Rather?* (page 14)

> copies of *Earth, Moon, and Sun—Meaningful Words* (page 15)

> copies of *Earth, Moon, and Sun—Wacky Writing* (page 16)

> copies of *Earth, Moon, and Sun—Say What? Extensions* (page 17)

> scissors and glue

Additional Figures of Speech

> down to earth
> heaven on earth
> salt of the earth
> nothing new under the sun
> fall off the face of the earth
> think someone hung the moon
> the sun rises and sets on someone
> never let the sun catch you sleeping

Answer Key

Match That Figure! (page 13)

1. going to sleep early, often when the sun goes down

2. very seldom; something that hardly ever happens

3. doing something when you have the opportunity

4. committing to someone you trust and love forever

5. extremely happy and pleased

Pictures will vary but should show an understanding for each figure of speech.

Would You Rather? (page 14)

Check sentences to be sure students' explanations answer the questions.

Meaningful Words (page 15)

1. B   2. A   3. B
Challenge: Check sentences to be sure contexts match the definitions chosen.
4. A   5. C   6. B
Challenge: Check sentences to be sure contexts match the definitions chosen.

Wacky Writing (page 16)

Students' responses should accurately answer each prompt and demonstrate understanding of the figurative phrase.

Say What? Extensions (page 17)

Check to see that students have completed two of the three activities.

Earth, Moon, and Sun—Match That Figure!

Directions: Cut apart the definition cards. Glue each definition next to the correct phrase. Then, draw a picture to represent each figurative phrase.

Phrases	Definitions	Pictures
1. go to bed with the sun (proverb)		
2. once in a blue moon (idiom)		
3. make hay while the sun shines (proverb)		
4. follow to the ends of the earth (idiom)		
5. over the moon (idiom)		

doing something when you have the opportunity	very seldom; something that hardly ever happens	extremely happy and pleased	going to sleep early, often when the sun goes down	committing to someone you trust and love forever

Earth, Moon, and Sun—Would You Rather?

Directions: Read and answer each question.

1. Would you rather follow a president or your best friend *to the ends of the earth*? Why?

   _____

   _____

   _____

2. Would you rather *go to bed with the sun* or wake up with the sun? Why?

   _____

   _____

   _____

3. Would you rather eat ice cream or spinach *once in a blue moon*? Why?

   _____

   _____

   _____

4. Would you rather be *over the moon* about giving gifts to people or receiving gifts from people? Why?

   _____

   _____

   _____

5. Write your own question using the phrase *make hay while the sun shines.*

   _____

   _____

   _____

Earth, Moon, and Sun—Meaningful Words

Directions: For each sentence, write the letter of the correct definition. Then, create your own sentence using the selected word.

| once in a **blue** moon | **A.** blue (adjective): a color, often described as a clear sky |
| | **B.** blue (adjective): feeling sad or down in spirits |

____ 1. Tim became blue when he noticed it might rain on his birthday.

____ 2. Melissa was excited to paint her room blue and turquoise.

____ 3. Jerry felt blue after he saw his poor grades on his report card.

Challenge: Choose a definition, and write a sentence using the word *blue*.

_____

_____

_____

make hay while the sun shines	**A.** shine (verb): the act of polishing an object to make it glisten
	B. shine (noun): the light coming off an object
	C. shine (verb): to be good at something and stand out

____ 4. Karen worked diligently trying to shine her shoes to be ready for the dance.

____ 5. Terry's skills in reading allowed her to shine in class and advance to chapter books.

____ 6. Julio was blinded by the shine coming off the newly painted car.

Challenge: Choose a definition, and write a sentence using the word *shines*.

_____

_____

_____

Earth, Moon, and Sun—Wacky Writing

Directions: Read and answer each prompt.

1. Describe two people you would *follow to the ends of the earth*. Then, explain why you would choose them.

   _____

   _____

   _____

2. Explain three benefits of *going to bed with the sun*.

   _____

   _____

   _____

3. Describe two things you only do *once in a blue moon*.

   _____

   _____

   _____

4. Write about something you could do to *make hay while the sun shines* if you had an extra hour each day.

   _____

   _____

   _____

5. Describe something you could receive in the mail that you would be *over the moon* about.

   _____

   _____

   _____

Earth, Moon, and Sun—Say What? Extensions

Directions: Choose two activities to complete.

> » follow to the ends of the earth   » once in a blue moon
>
> » go to bed with the sun   » over the moon
>
> » make hay while the sun shines

👓 Read All About It!

With a partner, pretend you work for a news organization and have to write one paragraph about something that happened in your town. The story should contain at least two of this week's figures of speech.

Mime Time

Take turns acting out all five of the figures of speech with your partner or group members. You may only act out the clues with body language and gestures. You may not use your voice!

🔫⋮ Say It, Don't Spray It!

Work with a small group to write and tell a story that includes all five figures of speech. One person begins the story. Then, each person takes a turn adding an idea to the story. Continue the story until all figures of speech have been used and the story comes to an end.

over the moon

Figures of Speech

» asleep at the wheel   » set the wheels in motion

» have a screw loose   » the squeaky wheel gets the oil

» put your shoulder to the wheel

Overview

Students will enjoy learning about forces- and motion-related figures of speech through the activities in this section. For detailed instructions on how to implement the activities in this lesson, see pages 8–10.

Materials

> copies of *Forces and Motion—Match That Figure!* (page 19)

> copies of *Forces and Motion— Would You Rather?* (page 20)

> copies of *Forces and Motion—Meaningful Words* (page 21)

> copies of *Forces and Motion—Wacky Writing* (page 22)

> copies of *Forces and Motion—Say What? Extensions* (page 23)

> scissors and glue

Additional Figures of Speech

> third/fifth wheel
> reinvent the wheel
> drive a wedge between
> throw a wrench in the works
> wedge in between something
> get your head screwed on straight

Answer Key

Match That Figure! (page 19)

1. people who talk or complain the most get what they want

2. to get started on a project or activity

3. to work with a lot of effort to accomplish a task

4. to act a little silly or crazy, sometimes seeming foolish

5. not paying attention to the task at hand

Pictures will vary but should show an understanding for each figure of speech.

Would You Rather? (page 20)

Check sentences to be sure students' explanations answer the questions.

Meaningful Words (page 21)

1. A   2. B   3. A
Challenge: Check sentences to be sure contexts match the definitions chosen.
4. B   5. B   6. A
Challenge: Check sentences to be sure contexts match the definitions chosen.

Wacky Writing (page 22)

Students' responses should accurately answer each prompt and demonstrate understanding of the figurative phrase.

Say What? Extensions (page 23)

Check to see that students have completed two of the three activities.

Name _____ Date _____

Forces and Motion—Match That Figure!

Directions: Cut apart the definition cards. Glue each definition next to the correct phrase. Then, draw a picture to represent each figurative phrase.

Phrases	Definitions	Pictures
1. the squeaky wheel gets the oil (proverb)		
2. set the wheels in motion (idiom)		
3. put your shoulder to the wheel (idiom)		
4. have a screw loose (idiom)		
5. asleep at the wheel (idiom)		

to get started on a project or activity	to act a little silly or crazy, sometimes seeming foolish	people who talk or complain the most get what they want	not paying attention to the task at hand	to work with a lot of effort to accomplish a task

Forces and Motion—Would You Rather?

Directions: Read and answer each question.

1. Would you rather *set the wheels in motion* to begin your own business or produce your own movie? Why?

   _____

   _____

   _____

2. Would you rather be *a squeaky wheel* or wait quietly when you want something? Why?

   _____

   _____

   _____

3. Would you rather be *asleep at the wheel* while in school or working at home? Why?

   _____

   _____

   _____

4. Would you rather procrastinate or *put your shoulder to the wheel* to get an important project completed? Why?

   _____

   _____

   _____

5. Write your own question using the phrase *have a screw loose*.

   _____

   _____

   _____

Forces and Motion—Meaningful Words

Directions: For each sentence, write the letter of the correct definition. Then, create your own sentence using the selected word.

set the wheels in motion	**A.** set (verb): to put something down in a particular place **B.** set (noun): a group of things that go together

____ 1. Lydia set the antique vase next to the auburn lamp on the coffee table.

____ 2. Dave grabbed his set of golf clubs from the closet before heading out the door.

____ 3. Brian set the baby down in the crib gently so he wouldn't wake up.

Challenge: Choose a definition, and write a sentence using the word *set*.

_____

_____

_____

_____

asleep at the wheel	**A.** wheel (noun): a circular shape **B.** wheel (verb): to cause to move, roll, or spin around

____ 4. The caterers wheeled out the appetizers just in time for the large, hungry crowd.

____ 5. Jackie wheeled around when she heard the loud banging in the hallway.

____ 6. Muhammad replaced the wheel on his bicycle because it was torn.

Challenge: Choose a definition, and write a sentence using the word *wheel*.

_____

_____

_____

_____

Forces and Motion—Wacky Writing

Directions: Read and answer each prompt.

1. Describe a time it would be bad to be *asleep at the wheel*.

   _____

   _____

   _____

2. Explain in what situation it would be good to *put your shoulder to the wheel*.

   _____

   _____

   _____

3. Describe a time when you were *the squeaky wheel* and *got the oil*.

   _____

   _____

   _____

4. Recount a time when you were a leader and *set the wheels in motion* on a task.

   _____

   _____

   _____

5. Describe a time when you thought someone *had a screw loose*. What was he or she doing?

   _____

   _____

   _____

Forces and Motion—Say What? Extension

Directions: Choose two activities to complete.

> » asleep at the wheel   » set the wheels in motion
>
> » have a screw loose   » the squeaky wheel gets the oil
>
> » put your shoulder to the wheel

 ## Figurative and Literal

Choose one figure of speech. Using a sheet of paper folded in half, write "literal" and "figurative" at the top of each side. Under "literal," draw your interpretation of the literal meaning of the figure of speech. Under "figurative," draw your interpretation of the figurative meaning of the figure of speech. Write the figure of speech on the back of your paper.

 ## Word Association

Choose one word to associate with each figure of speech. Then, find a partner and quiz each other to see who can solve which figures of speech are associated with the words you have chosen. For example, you can choose "storm" if the figure of speech is *it's raining cats and dogs*.

 ## Example and Non-Example

Choose one figure of speech. Then, write two sentences using the figure of speech appropriately and two using the figure of speech incorrectly. Read the four sentences to a partner and have him or her figure out which two sentences are good examples and which two sentences are non-examples.

have a screw loose

Figures of Speech

» between a rock and a hard place

» leave no stone unturned

» people who live in glass houses shouldn't throw stones

» carved in stone

» solid as a rock

Overview

Students will enjoy learning about rock- and stone-related figures of speech through the activities in this section. For detailed instructions on how to implement the activities in this lesson, see pages 8–10.

Materials

> copies of *Rocks and Stones—Match That Figure!* (page 25)

> copies of *Rocks and Stones— Would You Rather?* (page 26)

> copies of *Rocks and Stones—Meaningful Words* (page 27)

> copies of *Rocks and Stones—Wacky Writing* (page 28)

> copies of *Rocks and Stones—Say What? Extensions* (page 29)

> scissors and glue

Additional Figures of Speech

> on the rocks
> heart of stone
> stepping stones
> hit rock bottom
> stone's throw away
> kill two birds with one stone

Match That Figure! (page 25)

1. very dependable person
2. people should not criticize others for faults they have themselves
3. deciding between two unpleasant options
4. to exhaust every possibility in achieving a goal
5. something that is permanent

Pictures will vary but should show an understanding for each figure of speech.

Would You Rather? (page 26)

Check sentences to be sure students' explanations answer the questions.

Meaningful Words (page 27)

1. B   2. C   3. A
Challenge: Check sentences to be sure contexts match the definitions chosen.
4. B   5. B   6. A
Challenge: Check sentences to be sure contexts match the definitions chosen.

Wacky Writing (page 28)

Students' responses should accurately answer each prompt and demonstrate understanding of the figurative phrase.

Say What? Extensions (page 29)

Check to see that students have completed two of the three activities.

Rocks and Stones—Match That Figure!

Directions: Cut apart the definition cards. Glue each definition next to the correct phrase. Then, draw a picture to represent each figurative phrase.

Phrases	Definitions	Pictures
1. solid as a rock (idiom)		
2. people in glass houses shouldn't throw stones (idiom)		
3. between a rock and a hard place (idiom)		
4. leave no stone unturned (idiom)		
5. carved in stone (idiom)		

very dependable person	something that is permanent	to exhaust every possibility in achieving a goal	deciding between two unpleasant options	people should not criticize others for faults they have themselves

51626—Go Figure! Exploring Figurative Language

Rocks and Stones—Would You Rather?

Directions: Read and answer each question.

1. Following the idiom *between a rock and a hard place*, would you rather get an A in math or get a B while helping a friend do better? Why?

   _____

   _____

   _____

2. Would you rather *leave no stone unturned* looking for the perfect pair of jeans or the perfect pair of sunglasses? Why?

   _____

   _____

   _____

3. Would you rather have a best friend who is *solid as a rock* or a best friend who is sometimes not there to support you?

   _____

   _____

   _____

4. If a decision had to be *carved in stone*, would you rather have your parents choose your career or who you can date? Why?

   _____

   _____

   _____

5. Write your own question using the phrase *people who live in glass houses shouldn't throw stones*.

   _____

   _____

   _____

Rocks and Stones—Meaningful Words

Directions: For each sentence, write the letter of the correct definition. Then, create your own sentence using the selected word.

solid as a <u>rock</u>	**A.** rock (noun): a mass of mineral matter formed as a stone
	B. rock (verb): to move or sway back and forth
	C. rock (verb): to stir up

____ 1. Dario gently rocked his baby brother to sleep.

____ 2. The crowd was ready to rock as they waited for the artist to come on stage.

____ 3. Linda enjoyed finding rocks at the park to add to her growing collection.

Challenge: Choose a definition, and write a sentence using the word *rock*.

_____

_____

_____

| people who live in glass <u>houses</u> shouldn't throw stones | **A.** house (noun): a building in which people live, worship, or perform |
| | **B.** house (verb): to provide storage or shelter |

____ 4. The library was so large that it was able to house over a million books.

____ 5. To keep his apartment neat, Karl bought a new container to house his boots.

____ 6. The houses on the street were going to be torn down to build a new freeway.

Challenge: Choose a definition, and write a sentence using the word *houses*.

_____

_____

Rocks and Stones—Wacky Writing

Directions: Read and answer each prompt.

1. Describe three rules of friendship that you think should be *carved in stone*.

   _____

   _____

   _____

2. Share a time when you were *stuck between a rock and a hard place* and what you decided to do.

   _____

   _____

   _____

3. Name a time in which you *left no stone unturned* to accomplish a goal.

   _____

   _____

   _____

4. List five people in your life you think are *solid as a rock*.

   _____

   _____

   _____

5. Since *people who live in glass houses shouldn't throw stones*, name three things for which you would never criticize someone else.

   _____

   _____

   _____

Rocks and Stones—Say What? Extensions

Directions: Choose two activities to complete.

> » between a rock and a hard place » carved in stone
>
> » leave no stone unturned » solid as a rock
>
> » people who live in glass houses shouldn't throw stones

 ## Short Story

Write a short description of something that recently happened to you using two of the figures of speech. Be sure the figures of speech are used correctly. Underline them when you are finished.

 ## Poetry Time

Choose one of the figures of speech. Then, create a short poem or rap with eight lines that would help someone younger than you understand the meaning of the figure of speech. You can use the definition, examples, and your own creativity to make it fun and interesting.

 ## Friendly Letter

Write a friendly letter to someone who has always been *solid as a rock* in your life. Tell that person why you appreciate him or her. Be sure to use the phrase *solid as a rock* in your letter. If you have the chance, mail the letter to the recipient.

solid as a rock

Figures of Speech

» the darkest hour is just before dawn

» light a fire under

» haven't seen the light of day

» light at the end of the tunnel

» many hands make light work

Overview

Students will enjoy learning about light- and energy-related figures of speech through the activities in this section. For detailed instructions on how to implement the activities in this lesson, see pages 8–10.

Materials

> copies of *Light and Energy—Match That Figure!* (page 31)

> copies of *Light and Energy—Would You Rather?* (page 32)

> copies of *Light and Energy—Meaningful Words* (page 33)

> copies of *Light and Energy—Wacky Writing* (page 34)

> copies of *Light and Energy—Say What? Extensions* (page 35)

> scissors and glue

Additional Figures of Speech

> dark horse
> light years
> light as a feather
> keep someone in the dark

Answer Key

Match That Figure! (page 31)

1. being close to the end of a difficult task or situation
2. information that isn't available or known to most people
3. when things get really difficult, they might be about to turn around or improve
4. urge someone to work harder
5. if everyone helps with a large task, it gets finished easily and quickly

Pictures will vary but should show an understanding for each figure of speech.

Would You Rather? (page 32)

Check sentences to be sure students' explanations answer the questions.

Meaningful Words (page 33)

1. C   2. A   3. B

Challenge: Check sentences to be sure contexts match the definitions chosen.

4. B   5. A   6. C

Challenge: Check sentences to be sure contexts match the definitions chosen.

Wacky Writing (page 34)

Students' responses should accurately answer each prompt and demonstrate understanding of the figurative phrase.

Say What? Extensions (page 35)

Check to see that students have completed two of the three activities.

Light and Energy—Match That Figure!

Directions: Cut apart the definition cards. Glue each definition next to the correct phrase. Then, draw a picture to represent each figurative phrase.

Phrases	Definitions	Pictures
1. light at the end of the tunnel (idiom)		
2. haven't seen the light of day (idiom)		
3. the darkest hour is just before dawn (proverb)		
4. light a fire under (idiom)		
5. many hands make light work (proverb)		

when things get really difficult, they might be about to turn around or improve	if everyone helps with a large task, it gets finished easily and quickly	information that is not available or known to most people	being close to the end of a difficult task or situation	urge someone to work harder

Light and Energy—Would You Rather?

Directions: Read and answer each question.

1. Would you rather have your report card *see the light of day* or disappear forever? Why?

   _____

   _____

   _____

2. Would you rather have your parents or your friends *light a fire under you* to get your homework done? Why?

   _____

   _____

   _____

3. Would you rather see a *light at the end of the tunnel* or quit a task while no one is watching? Why?

   _____

   _____

   _____

4. Since *many hands make light work*, would you rather be in charge of delegating the task or be the worker delegated a big task? Why?

   _____

   _____

   _____

5. Write your own question using the phrase *the darkest hour is just before dawn*.

   _____

   _____

   _____

Light and Energy—Meaningful Words

Directions: For each sentence, write the letter of the correct definition. Then, create your own sentence using the selected word.

light a <u>fire</u> under	**A.** fire (noun): a burning material
	B. fire (verb): to start up
	C. fire (verb): to terminate someone's employment

____ 1. Due to the company losing funding, it had to fire half its employees.

____ 2. The snow falling outside called for the first fire of the season in the fireplace.

____ 3. Larry fired up the computer to start on his project.

Challenge: Choose a definition, and write a sentence using the word *fire*.

_____

_____

_____

many hands make <u>light</u> work	**A.** light (noun): an illuminating source
	B. light (adjective): pale in color
	C. light (verb): to ignite or set to burn

____ 4. The school children could see the storm turn the light blue sky dark gray.

____ 5. The light from the new bulb was so strong Sarah had to squint.

____ 6. There was a power outage in her town, and Felicia was forced to light candles.

Challenge: Choose a definition, and write a sentence using the word *light*.

_____

_____

Light and Energy—Wacky Writing

Directions: Read and answer each prompt.

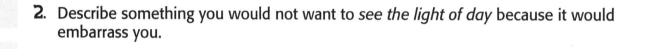

1. Explain a task for which you would need someone to *light a fire under* you to complete.

   _____

   _____

   _____

2. Describe something you would not want to *see the light of day* because it would embarrass you.

   _____

   _____

   _____

3. Describe a time when you felt like you were experiencing the *darkest hour just before dawn.*

   _____

   _____

   _____

4. Name three household chores that you would accept help to do since *many hands make light work.*

   _____

   _____

   _____

5. Describe something that took a long time for you to finish and at what point you saw the *light at the end of the tunnel.*

   _____

   _____

   _____

Light and Energy—Say What? Extensions

Directions: Choose two activities to complete.

> » light at the end of the tunnel
> » haven't seen the light of day
> » the darkest hour is just before dawn
> » light a fire under
> » many hands make light work

Tunnel Vision

Illustrate an example of the phrase *light at the end of the tunnel*. Draw a large tunnel on a piece of paper. At the end of the tunnel, write down a goal you recently accomplished. Then, list everything you had to do to reach this goal along the walls of the tunnel. Finally, underline the event, or "light," that helped you know you were close to accomplishing your goal.

Comic Strip

Create a short four- to six-frame comic strip with sketches or simple pictures. Show the humor of one character using a figure of speech and the other character taking it literally.

Actor's Studio

In a small group, brainstorm five additional figures of speech. Write this week's figures of speech and the five additional figures of speech on small slips of paper. Then, divide into two teams and play a short game of charades using the figures of speech as the secret phrases.

light a fire under

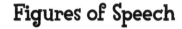

Figures of Speech

» make something up out of whole cloth

» break new ground

» teach an old dog new tricks

» necessity is the mother of invention

» reinvent the wheel

Overview

Students will enjoy learning about invention-related figures of speech through the activities in this section. For detailed instructions on how to implement the activities in this lesson, see pages 8–10.

Materials

> copies of *Invention—Match That Figure!* (page 37)
> copies of *Invention—Would You Rather?* (page 38)
> copies of *Invention—Meaningful Words* (page 39)
> copies of *Invention—Wacky Writing* (page 40)
> copies of *Invention—Say What? Extensions* (page 41)
> scissors and glue
> index cards

Additional Figures of Speech

> create a stir
> create a stink
> create an uproar
> that's a new one
> a new slant on something

Answer Key

Match That Figure! (page 37)

1. you are more likely to figure out how to do something when you really need to

2. to create something that someone else already has

3. it's difficult to try and change someone's longtime habits or teach him or her a new skill

4. to invent a complete story or explanation from nothing

5. to start or invent something nobody else has before

Pictures will vary but should show an understanding for each figure of speech.

Would You Rather? (page 38)

Check sentences to be sure students' explanations answer the questions.

Meaningful Words (page 39)

1. A   2. A   3. B
Challenge: Check sentences to be sure contexts match the definitions chosen.
4. A   5. B   6. A
Challenge: Check sentences to be sure contexts match the definitions chosen.

Wacky Writing (page 40)

Students' responses should accurately answer each prompt and demonstrate understanding of the figurative phrase.

Say What? Extensions (page 41)

Check to see that students have completed two of the three activities.

Invention—Match That Figure!

Directions: Cut apart the definition cards. Glue each definition next to the correct phrase. Then, draw a picture to represent each figurative phrase.

Phrases	Definitions	Pictures
1. necessity is the mother of invention (proverb)		
2. reinvent the wheel (idiom)		
3. you can't teach an old dog new tricks (proverb)		
4. make something up out of whole cloth (idiom)		
5. break new ground (idiom)		

to start or invent something nobody else has before	it's difficult to try and change someone's longtime habits or teach him or her a new skill	you are more likely to figure out how to do something when you really need to	to create something that someone else already has	to invent a complete story or explanation from nothing

Invention—Would You Rather?

Directions: Read and answer each question.

1. Would you rather *reinvent the wheel* and design your own MP3 player or buy one someone else designed? Why?

   _____

   _____

   _____

2. Would you rather have to *teach an old dog new tricks* by yourself or with a friend? Why?

   _____

   _____

   _____

3. If your best friend was in trouble, would you rather *make something up out of whole cloth* to protect him or her, or tell the truth? Why?

   _____

   _____

   _____

4. Would you rather *break new ground* by writing your own song or creating a new sport? Why?

   _____

   _____

   _____

5. Write your own question using the phrase *necessity is the mother of invention*.

   _____

   _____

   _____

Invention—Meaningful Words

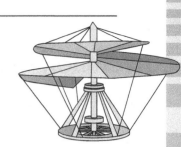

Directions: For each sentence, write the letter of the correct definition. Then, create your own sentence using the selected word.

necessity is the <u>mother</u> of invention	**A.** mother (noun): a female parent
	B. mother (verb): to care for

____ 1. My mother and grandfather came with me to every dance practice.

____ 2. Her instinct as a mother kicked in so she checked in on her son at the party.

____ 3. The cat mothered her five kittens by bathing them with her own tongue.

Challenge: Choose a definition, and write a sentence using the word *mother*.

_____

_____

_____

_____

you can't teach an old dog new <u>tricks</u>	**A.** trick (noun): a prank or stunt to fool someone
	B. trick (noun): a clever or ingenious technique

____ 4. The magician stunned the audience with a complicated trick.

____ 5. Paul showed off the new tricks he learned on his skateboard.

____ 6. Julia always played funny tricks on her younger sister.

Challenge: Choose a definition, and write a sentence using the word *tricks*.

_____

_____

_____

Invention—Wacky Writing

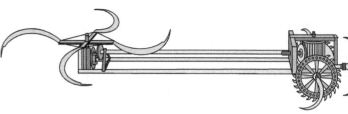

Directions: Read and answer each prompt.

1. Describe a time when you felt you were trying to *teach an old dog new tricks*.

   _____

   _____

   _____

2. Name three things you used this morning on which you wouldn't waste your time *reinventing the wheel* and re-creating your own.

   _____

   _____

   _____

3. Describe a time you *broke new ground* and came up with an idea that nobody had ever thought of before.

   _____

   _____

   _____

4. Share a time you needed to *make something up out of whole cloth* to avoid getting in trouble for something you had done.

   _____

   _____

   _____

5. Describe a time when you had to figure out how to do something right on the spot because *necessity is the mother of invention*.

   _____

   _____

   _____

Invention—Say What? Extensions

Directions: Choose two activities to complete.

> » make something up out of whole cloth
>
> » break new ground
>
> » teach an old dog new tricks
>
> » necessity is the mother of invention
>
> » reinvent the wheel

 ## Matching Game

Create a matching game with a partner. Using 10 index cards, write each figure of speech on one card and your own definition for each phrase on another card. Mix up all the cards. Time how long it takes you to match each figure of speech with its definition. Have your partner try to beat your time. Each person goes twice to see who can achieve the fastest time.

 ## Comic Strip

Create a short four- to six-frame comic strip with sketches or simple pictures. Show the humor of one character using a figure of speech and the other character taking it literally.

 ## Conversation Starter

Create a dialogue between you and a friend using at least three figures of speech. Write down your conversation.

reinvent the wheel

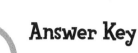

Figures of Speech

» go off in different directions

» put something on the map

» wait until the coast is clear

» move mountains

» no man is an island

Overview

Students will enjoy learning about geography-related figures of speech through the activities in this section. For detailed instructions on how to implement the activities in this lesson, see pages 8–10.

Materials

> copies of *Geography—Match That Figure!* (page 43)
> copies of *Geography—Would You Rather?* (page 44)
> copies of *Geography—Meaningful Words* (page 45)
> copies of *Geography—Wacky Writing* (page 46)
> copies of *Geography—Say What? Extensions* (page 47)
> scissors and glue

Additional Figures of Speech

> test the waters
> live off the land
> dead in the water
> fish in troubled waters
> a step in the right direction
> the tide has turned

Answer Key

Match That Figure! (page 43)

1. two or more people having different ideas of how to do something

2. human beings must depend on each other for some things

3. achieving something that is very difficult

4. wait until there is no visible danger before doing something

5. to make a person, place, or thing famous or popular

Pictures will vary but should show an understanding for each figure of speech.

Would You Rather? (page 44)

Check sentences to be sure students' explanations answer the questions.

Meaningful Words (page 45)

1. A   2. B   3. B
Challenge: Check sentences to be sure contexts match the definitions chosen.
4. C   5. A   6. B
Challenge: Check sentences to be sure contexts match the definitions chosen.

Wacky Writing (page 46)

Students' responses should accurately answer each prompt and demonstrate understanding of the figurative phrase.

Say What? Extensions (page 47)

Check to see that students have completed two of the three activities.

Geography—Match That Figure!

Directions: Cut apart the definition cards. Glue each definition next to the correct phrase. Then, draw a picture to represent each figurative phrase.

Figures of speech	Definitions	Pictures
1. go off in different directions (idiom)		
2. no man is an island (proverb)		
3. move mountains (idiom)		
4. wait until the coast is clear (idiom)		
5. put something on the map (idiom)		

human beings must depend on each other for some things	wait until there is no visible danger before doing something	to make a person, place, or thing famous or popular	achieving something that is very difficult	two or more people having different ideas of how to do something

Geography—Would You Rather?

Directions: Read and answer each question.

1. Would you rather make your friends or yourself famous by *putting either you or them on the map*? Why?

   _____

   _____

   _____

2. Would you rather *move mountains* for something or for someone you feel strongly about? Why?

   _____

   _____

   _____

3. Would you rather *go off in a different direction* by wearing a unique hairstyle or a unique outfit? Why?

   _____

   _____

   _____

4. Would you rather *wait until the coast is clear* to open a Christmas present early or sneak a piece of cake? Why?

   _____

   _____

   _____

5. Write your own question using the phrase *no man is an island*.

   _____

   _____

   _____

Geography—Meaningful Words

Directions: For each sentence, write the letter of the correct definition. Then, create your own sentence using the selected word.

wait until the <u>coast</u> is clear	**A.** coast (noun): the land near a sea **B.** coast (verb): to slide or go down an incline with little to no effort

____ 1. While vacationing in Hawaii, Wayne and Sarah took a drive near the coast.

____ 2. After slowly trudging up the steep road on her bicycle, Trudy coasted down the other side and enjoyed the wind blowing on her face.

____ 3. The expert skier coasted down the hill on her skis and won first place.

Challenge: Choose a definition, and write a sentence using the word *coast*.

_____

_____

_____

wait until the coast is <u>clear</u>	**A.** clear (adjective): transparent or without color **B.** clear (verb): to clean off or remove objects **C.** clear (adjective): easy to understand or hear

____ 4. The flight attendant gave clear directions to the passengers boarding the plane.

____ 5. The woman's clear glasses turned to sunglasses when she walked outside.

____ 6. The Girl Scouts cleared off the table to begin working on their project.

Challenge: Choose a definition, and write a sentence using the word *clear*.

_____

_____

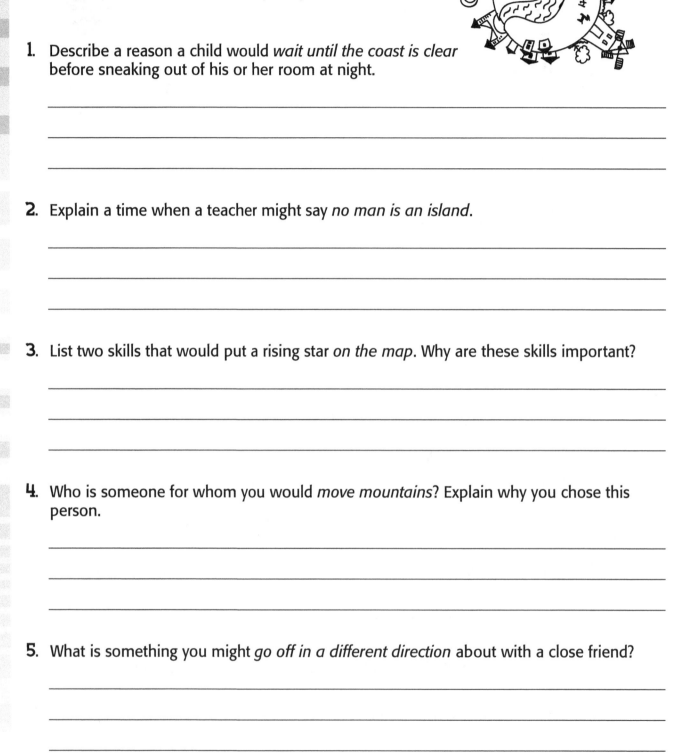

Geography—Wacky Writing

Directions: Read and answer each prompt.

1. Describe a reason a child would *wait until the coast is clear* before sneaking out of his or her room at night.

   _____

   _____

   _____

2. Explain a time when a teacher might say *no man is an island*.

   _____

   _____

   _____

3. List two skills that would put a rising star *on the map*. Why are these skills important?

   _____

   _____

   _____

4. Who is someone for whom you would *move mountains*? Explain why you chose this person.

   _____

   _____

   _____

5. What is something you might *go off in a different direction* about with a close friend?

   _____

   _____

   _____

Geography—Say What? Extensions

Directions: Choose two activities to complete.

> » go off in different directions   » move mountains
>
> » put something on the map   » no man is an island
>
> » wait until the coast is clear

No Man Is an Island

Create a story about what you would do if you were on a deserted island. What would your experience be like? How would you feel about being alone? Use at least one figure of speech in your story. Share your story with a partner.

Poetry Time

Choose one of the figures of speech. Then, create a short poem or rap with eight lines that would help someone younger than you understand the meaning of the figure of speech. You can use the definition, examples, and your own creativity to make it fun and interesting.

Figurative and Literal

Choose one figure of speech. Using a sheet of paper folded in half, write "literal" and "figurative" at the top of each side. Under "literal," draw your interpretation of the literal meaning of the figure of speech. Under "figurative," draw your interpretation of the figurative meaning of the figure of speech. Write the figure of speech on the back of your paper.

put something on the map

Figures of Speech

» sell a bill of goods

» laugh all the way to the bank

» a friend in need is a friend indeed

» break the bank

» in short supply

Overview

Students will enjoy learning about economics-related figures of speech through the activities in this section. For detailed instructions on how to implement the activities in this lesson, see pages 8–10.

Materials

> copies of *Economics—Match That Figure!* (page 49)

> copies of *Economics—Would You Rather?* (page 50)

> copies of *Economics—Meaningful Words* (page 51)

> copies of *Economics—Wacky Writing* (page 52)

> copies of *Economics—Say What? Extensions* (page 53)

> scissors and glue

Additional Figures of Speech

> buy the farm

> sell your soul

> false economy

> in great demand

> take it to the bank

> bank on something

Answer Key

Match That Figure! (page 49)

1. earning money for something someone else thinks you don't deserve

2. buying something so expensive that it uses up all of your money

3. get someone to believe something that isn't true

4. to be willing to do anything for someone you care about

5. having a small amount of something

Pictures will vary but should show an understanding for each figure of speech.

Would You Rather? (page 50)

Check sentences to be sure students' explanations answer the questions.

Meaningful Words (page 51)

1. C   2. B   3. A

Challenge: Check sentences to be sure contexts match the definitions chosen.

4. A   5. A   6. B

Challenge: Check sentences to be sure contexts match the definitions chosen.

Wacky Writing (page 52)

Students' responses should accurately answer each prompt and demonstrate understanding of the figurative phrase.

Say What? Extensions (page 53)

Check to see that students have completed two of the three activities.

Economics—Match That Figure!

Directions: Cut apart the definition cards. Glue each definition next to the correct phrase. Then, draw a picture to represent each figurative phrase.

Figures of speech	Definitions	Pictures
1. laugh all the way to the bank (idiom)		
2. break the bank (idiom)		
3. sell a bill of goods (idiom)		
4. a friend in need is a friend indeed (idiom)		
5. in short supply (idiom)		

get someone to believe something that isn't true	earning money for something someone else thinks you don't deserve	to be willing to do anything for someone you care about	buying something so expensive that it uses up all of your money	having a small amount of something

Economics—Would You Rather?

Directions: Read and answer each question.

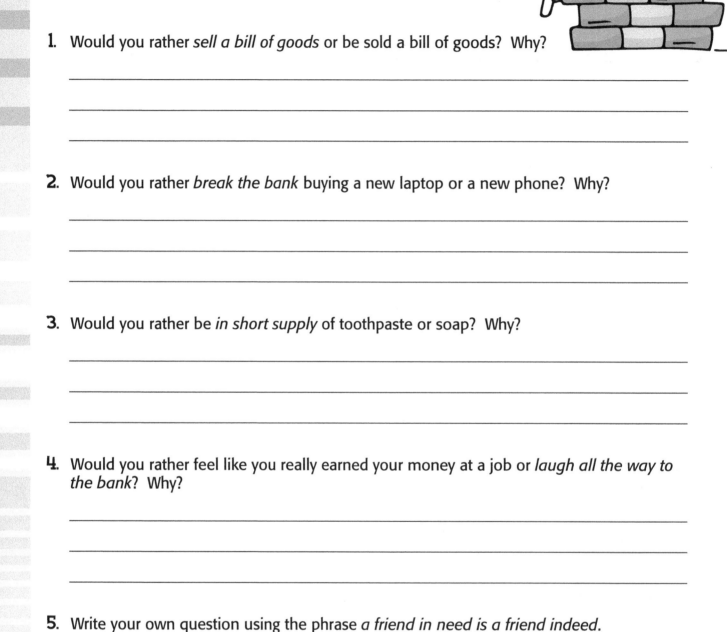

1. Would you rather *sell a bill of goods* or be sold a bill of goods? Why?

   _____

   _____

   _____

2. Would you rather *break the bank* buying a new laptop or a new phone? Why?

   _____

   _____

   _____

3. Would you rather be *in short supply* of toothpaste or soap? Why?

   _____

   _____

   _____

4. Would you rather feel like you really earned your money at a job or *laugh all the way to the bank*? Why?

   _____

   _____

   _____

5. Write your own question using the phrase *a friend in need is a friend indeed*.

   _____

   _____

   _____

Economics—Meaningful Words

Directions: For each sentence, write the letter of the correct definition.
Then, create your own sentence using the selected word.

break the <u>bank</u>	**A.** bank (noun): a place where people keep or borrow money **B.** bank (noun): the slope of a hill **C.** bank (verb): to rely on or earn something to use later

____ 1. Our team banked on Jesse scoring the most points during the final game.

____ 2. Brendon fell down the muddy bank because his shoes were too slippery.

____ 3. Stopping by the bank to get cash made us late for the movie.

Challenge: Choose a definition, and write a sentence using the word *bank*.

_____

_____

_____

sell a <u>bill</u> of goods	**A.** bill (noun): a statement of money owed for goods or services **B.** bill (noun): a piece of paper money

____ 4. After dinner and dessert, the waiter brought our bill to the table.

____ 5. Susan's air conditioning bill is always higher during the summer months.

____ 6. Maria handed the cashier a crisp twenty-dollar bill for her groceries.

Challenge: Choose a definition, and write a sentence using the word *bill*.

_____

_____

_____

Economics—Wacky Writing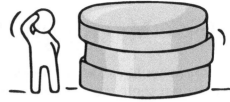

Directions: Read and answer each prompt.

1. Explain why someone would try to *sell a bill of goods* to someone else.

   _____

   _____

   _____

2. List two purchases by you or your parents that would *break the bank*.

   _____

   _____

   _____

3. Describe a time when you demonstrated that *a friend in need is a friend indeed*.

   _____

   _____

   _____

4. Name a time you earned money easily and *laughed all the way to the bank*.

   _____

   _____

   _____

5. Describe a time when someone you know was *in short supply* of common sense and made a bad decision.

   _____

   _____

   _____

Economics—Say What? Extensions

Directions: Choose two activities to complete.

> » sell a bill of goods
>
> » laugh all the way to the bank
>
> » a friend in need is a friend indeed
>
> » break the bank
>
> » in short supply

 ## Word Association

Choose one word to associate with each figure of speech. Then, find a partner and quiz each other to see who can solve which figures of speech are associated with the words you have chosen. For example, you can choose "storm" if the figure of speech is *it's raining cats and dogs*.

 ## Say It, Don't Spray It!

Work with a small group to write and tell a story that includes all five figures of speech. One person begins the story. Then, each person takes a turn adding an idea to the story. Continue the story until all figures of speech have been used and the story comes to an end.

 ## Actor's Studio

In a small group, brainstorm five additional figures of speech. Write this week's figures of speech and the five additional figures of speech on small slips of paper. Then, divide into two teams and play a short game of charades using the figures of speech as the secret phrases.

break the bank

Figures of Speech

- » fight fire with fire
- » war of words
- » battle of wills
- » fight like cats and dogs
- » if you want to make peace, prepare for war

Overview

Students will enjoy learning about war- and battle-related figures of speech through the activities in this section. For detailed instructions on how to implement the activities in this lesson, see pages 8–10.

Materials

- › copies of *Wars and Battles—Match That Figure!* (page 55)
- › copies of *Wars and Battles—Would You Rather?* (page 56)
- › copies of *Wars and Battles—Meaningful Words* (page 57)
- › copies of *Wars and Battles—Wacky Writing* (page 58)
- › copies of *Wars and Battles—Say What? Extensions* (page 59)
- › scissors and glue
- › index cards

Additional Figures of Speech

- › go to war
- › battle cry
- › uphill battle
- › fighting chance
- › draw battle lines
- › come out swinging
- › fight the good fight
- › fight your own battle

Answer Key

Match That Figure! (page 55)

1. a long verbal argument between two people or groups
2. to argue vigorously
3. an enemy is less likely to attack if you are prepared for battle
4. use the same method your opponent is using to fight against you
5. a situation in which opposing sides are equally determined to win

Pictures will vary but should show an understanding for each figure of speech.

Would You Rather? (page 56)

Check sentences to be sure students' explanations answer the questions.

Meaningful Words (page 57)

1. B   2. B   3. A
Challenge: Check sentences to be sure contexts match the definitions chosen.
4. A   5. B   6. A
Challenge: Check sentences to be sure contexts match the definitions chosen.

Wacky Writing (page 58)

Students' responses should accurately answer each prompt and demonstrate understanding of the figurative phrase.

Say What? Extensions (page 59)

Check to see that students have completed two of the three activities.

Wars and Battles—Match That Figure!

Directions: Cut apart the definition cards. Glue each definition next to the correct phrase. Then, draw a picture to represent each figurative phrase.

Figures of speech	Definitions	Pictures
1. war of words (idiom)		
2. fight like cats and dogs (idiom)		
3. if you want to make peace, prepare for war (proverb)		
4. fight fire with fire (idiom)		
5. battle of wills (idiom)		

to argue vigorously	use the same method your opponent is using to fight against you	a long verbal argument between two people or groups	an enemy is less likely to attack if you are prepared for battle	a situation in which opposing sides are equally determined to win

Wars and Battles—Would You Rather?

Directions: Read and answer each question.

1. Would you rather *fight like cats and dogs* with a sibling or a friend? Why?

   _____

   _____

   _____

2. Would you rather be polite to someone who has been mean to you or *fight fire with fire*? Why?

   _____

   _____

   _____

3. Would you rather have a *war of words* with your best friend or a sibling? Why?

   _____

   _____

   _____

4. Would you rather have *a battle of wills* with your teacher or your parents? Why?

   _____

   _____

   _____

5. Write your own question using the phrase *if you want to make peace, prepare for war*.

   _____

   _____

   _____

Wars and Battles—Meaningful Words

Directions: For each sentence, write the letter of the correct definition.
Then, create your own sentence using the selected word.

| **fight** fire with fire | **A.** fight (noun): a battle or struggle |
| | **B.** fight (verb): to engage in combat or struggle |

____ 1. Marc and Lila always fight over the remote controller after school.

____ 2. Dean did not want to see his best friends fight, so he intervened.

____ 3. Whenever the neighbors discuss politics, they end up in a fight.

Challenge: Choose a definition, and write a sentence using the word *fight*.

_____

_____

_____

| **battle** of wills | **A.** battle (noun): a conflict between two or more parties |
| | **B.** battle (verb): to engage in a conflict with another party |

____ 4. Union and Confederate forces fought the Battle of Gettysburg during the American Civil War.

____ 5. Our football team battled its rivals to win the victory trophy.

____ 6. The dodge ball battle finally ended with a tie.

Challenge: Choose a definition, and write a sentence using the word *battle*.

_____

_____

_____

Wars and Battles—Wacky Writing

Directions: Read and answer each prompt.

1. Discuss whether or not *if you want to make peace, prepare for war* is good advice to follow.

   _____

   _____

   _____

2. Share a time when you began a *war of words* with someone. Who won?

   _____

   _____

   _____

3. Do you believe *fighting fire with fire* is a mature way of handling an argument? Why or why not?

   _____

   _____

   _____

4. Describe a time when you had a *battle of wills* with someone. Why did you feel so strongly about your beliefs?

   _____

   _____

   _____

5. Share a time when you were younger and *fought like cats and dogs* with a sibling or a friend.

   _____

   _____

   _____

Wars and Battles—Say What? Extensions

Directions: Choose two activities to complete.

> » war of words   » fight fire with fire
>
> » battle of wills   » fight like cats and dogs
>
> » if you want to make peace, prepare for war

 ## Short Story

Write a short description of something that recently happened to you using two of the figures of speech. Be sure the figures of speech are used correctly. Underline them when you are finished.

👓 Read All About It!

With a partner, pretend you work for a news organization and have to write one paragraph about something that happened in your town. The story should contain at least two of this week's figures of speech.

 ## Matching Game

Create a matching game with a partner. Using 10 index cards, write each figure of speech on one card and your own definition for each phrase on another card. Mix up all the cards. Time how long it takes you to match each figure of speech with its definition. Have your partner try to beat your time. Each person goes twice to see who can achieve the fastest time.

fight like cats and dogs

51626—Go Figure! Exploring Figurative Language   **59**

Figures of Speech

» all roads lead to Rome

» it's all Greek to me

» bull in a china shop

» Rome wasn't built in a day

» when in Rome, do as the Romans do

Overview

Students will enjoy learning about ancient-civilization- and land- related figures of speech through the activities in this section. For detailed instructions on how to implement the activities in this lesson, see pages 8–10.

Materials

> copies of *Ancient Civilizations and Lands—Match That Figure!* (page 61)

> copies of *Ancient Civilizations and Lands—Would You Rather?* (page 62)

> copies of *Ancient Civilizations and Lands—Meaningful Words* (page 63)

> copies of *Ancient Civilizations and Lands—Wacky Writing* (page 64)

> copies of *Ancient Civilizations and Lands—Say What? Extensions* (page 65)

> scissors and glue

Additional Figures of Speech

> slow boat to China

> fiddle while Rome burns

> not for all the tea in China

> beware of Greeks bearing gifts

Answer Key

Match That Figure! (page 61)

1. something to say if you don't understand what someone is saying
2. there are many different routes to the same goal
3. someone who is clumsy in a delicate situation
4. it takes a long time to do something that is important
5. when with a new group of people, follow their ways of doing things

Pictures will vary but should show an understanding for each figure of speech.

Would You Rather? (page 62)

Check sentences to be sure students' explanations answer the questions.

Meaningful Words (page 63)

1. A   2. B   3. C

Challenge: Check sentences to be sure contexts match the definitions chosen.

4. B   5. A   6. B

Challenge: Check sentences to be sure contexts match the definitions chosen.

Wacky Writing (page 64)

Students' responses should accurately answer each prompt and demonstrate understanding of the figurative phrase.

Say What? Extensions (page 65)

Check to see that students have completed two of the three activities.

Ancient Civilizations and Lands—Match That Figure!

Directions: Cut apart the definition cards. Glue each definition next to the correct phrase. Then, draw a picture to represent each figurative phrase.

Figures of speech	Definitions	Pictures
1. it's all Greek to me (idiom)		
2. all roads lead to Rome (proverb)		
3. bull in a china shop (idiom)		
4. Rome wasn't built in a day (proverb)		
5. when in Rome, do as the Romans do (proverb)		

it takes a long time to do something that is important	there are many different routes to the same goal	when with a new group of people, follow their ways of doing things	someone who is clumsy in a delicate situation	something to say if you don't understand what someone is saying

Ancient Civilizations and Lands—Would You Rather?

Directions: Read and answer each question.

1. Would you rather knock over an entire display case of cheap items or one very expensive item while acting like a *bull in a china shop*? Why?

   _____

   _____

   _____

2. Considering the phrase *when in Rome, do as the Romans do*, would you rather eat the local cuisine in a foreign country or stick to food you've tried before? Why?

   _____

   _____

   _____

3. Would you rather solve a math problem using your teacher's method or your own, considering the phrase *all roads lead to Rome*? Why?

   _____

   _____

   _____

4. Would you rather try speaking or writing a foreign language that is *all Greek to you*? Why?

   _____

   _____

   _____

5. Write your own question using the phrase *Rome wasn't built in a day*.

   _____

   _____

   _____

Ancient Civilizations and Lands—Meaningful Words

Directions: For each sentence, write the letter of the correct definition. Then, create your own sentence using the selected word.

all roads <u>lead</u> to Rome	**A.** lead (verb): to physically go before and show the way down a path
	B. lead (verb): to be in charge of a group of people
	C. lead (noun): position at the front

____ 1. The guide had to lead us in the right direction so we didn't get lost on the hike.

____ 2. Jamie volunteered to be the lead in the group project for school.

____ 3. Nick took the lead in the race when another runner lost his footing.

Challenge: Choose a definition, and write a sentence using the word *lead*.

_____

_____

_____

| bull in a china <u>shop</u> | **A.** shop (noun): a retail store, often small |
| | **B.** shop (verb): to visit stores and purchase items |

____ 4. Cierra loved to shop at the mall when there was a clearance sale on jeans.

____ 5. The donut shop's sales increased as word spread about their delicious items.

____ 6. During the holidays, my grandma likes to shop online for gifts.

Challenge: Choose a definition, and write a sentence using the word *shop*.

_____

_____

_____

Social Studies > Name _____ Date _____

Ancient Civilizations and Lands—Wacky Writing

Directions: Read and answer each prompt.

1. Describe a project you worked on for a long time that proved the proverb *Rome wasn't built in a day.*

   _____
   _____
   _____

2. Name two different places you can work on your homework, proving the idiom *all roads lead to Rome.*

   _____
   _____
   _____

3. Name three topics that you know little about and could say *it's all Greek to me.*

   _____
   _____
   _____

4. Describe a time you felt like a *bull in a china shop.* Where were you?

   _____
   _____
   _____

5. Describe somewhere you want to visit and learn the local customs because *when in Rome, do as the Romans do.*

   _____
   _____
   _____

Ancient Civilizations and Lands—Say What? Extensions

Directions: Choose two activities to complete.

> » all roads lead to Rome
> » it's all Greek to me
>
> » bull in a china shop
> » Rome wasn't built in a day
>
> » when in Rome, do as the Romans do

 ## Mime Time

Take turns acting out all five of the figures of speech with your partner or group members. You may only act out the clues with body language and gestures. You may not use your voice!

 ## Example and Non-Example

Choose one figure of speech. Then, write two sentences using the figure of speech appropriately and two using the figure of speech incorrectly. Read the four sentences to a partner and have him or her figure out which two sentences are good examples and which two sentences are non-examples.

 ## Comic Strip

Create a short four- to six-frame comic strip with sketches or simple pictures. Show the humor of one character using a figure of speech and the other character taking it literally.

bull in a china shop

51626—Go Figure! Exploring Figurative Language

Figures of Speech

» fall from grace

» King's ransom

» fit for a King

» live like a king

» the long arm of the law

Overview

Students will enjoy learning about ruler- and power-related figures of speech through the activities in this section. For detailed instructions on how to implement the activities in this lesson, see pages 8–10.

Materials

> copies of *Rulers and Power—Match That Figure!* (page 67)

> copies of *Rulers and Power—Would You Rather?* (page 68)

> copies of *Rulers and Power—Meaningful Words* (page 69)

> copies of *Rulers and Power—Wacky Writing* (page 70)

> copies of *Rulers and Power—Say What? Extensions* (page 71)

> scissors and glue

Additional Figures of Speech

> power trip

> cash is king

> kings have long arms

> build castles in the sky

> your home is your castle

> power behind the throne

Answer Key

Match That Figure! (page 67)

1. a term that refers to those who make and enforce laws

2. something that is very nice and luxurious

3. to go out of power, office, or a high-ranking job

4. a large amount of money

5. living a full and lavish life

Pictures will vary but should show an understanding for each figure of speech.

Would You Rather? (page 68)

Check sentences to be sure students' explanations answer the questions.

Meaningful Words (page 69)

1. A   2. A   3. B

Challenge: Check sentences to be sure contexts match the definitions chosen.

4. B   5. A   6. A

Challenge: Check sentences to be sure contexts match the definitions chosen.

Wacky Writing (page 70)

Students' responses should accurately answer each prompt and demonstrate understanding of the figurative phrase.

Say What? Extensions (page 71)

Check to see that students have completed two of the three activities.

Rulers and Power—Match That Figure!

Directions: Cut apart the definition cards. Glue each definition next to the correct phrase. Then, draw a picture to represent each figurative phrase.

Figures of speech	Definitions	Pictures
1. the long arm of the law (idiom)		
2. fit for a king (idiom)		
3. fall from grace (idiom)		
4. king's ransom (idiom)		
5. live like a king (proverb)		

to go out of power, office, or a high-ranking job	living a full and lavish life	a term that refers to those who make and enforce laws	a large amount of money	something that is very nice and luxurious

51626—Go Figure! Exploring Figurative Language

Rulers and Power—Would You Rather?

Directions: Read and answer each question.

1. Would you rather have power but *fall from grace* or never be in power in the first place? Why?

   _____

   _____

   _____

2. Would you rather move to a new location or stay at home if you had a *king's ransom*? Why?

   _____

   _____

   _____

3. Would you rather have a bedroom or a wardrobe *fit for a king*? Why?

   _____

   _____

   _____

4. Would you rather *live like a king* on your own island or in a lavish home? Why?

   _____

   _____

   _____

5. Write your own question using the phrase *long arm of the law*.

   _____

   _____

   _____

Rulers and Power—Meaningful Words

Directions: For each sentence, write the letter of the correct definition. Then, create your own sentence using the selected word.

| long <u>arm</u> of the law | **A.** arm (noun): an upper limb on a human body from the shoulder to the wrist |
| | **B.** arm (noun): an extension of an object that sticks out |

_____ 1. He had a bad sunburn on his arms after falling asleep at the beach.

_____ 2. My arms were sore after a hard workout at the gym.

_____ 3. Sal almost fell over when he sat down on the arm of the couch.

Challenge: Choose a definition, and write a sentence using the word *arm*.

_____

_____

_____

| <u>fall</u> from power | **A.** fall (verb): to drop down, usually accidentally from lack of support |
| | **B.** fall (noun): the season before winter; also known as autumn |

_____ 4. The red and orange leaves of fall looked like art in the front yard.

_____ 5. I watched the snow fall as I sat inside, snuggled under a blanket on the couch.

_____ 6. Her hair falls to her shoulders now that she cut it.

Challenge: Choose a definition, and write a sentence using the word *fall*.

_____

_____

_____

Rulers and Power—Wacky Writing

Directions: Read and answer each prompt.

1. Describe a historical figure who *fell from grace*. Who was it, and what did he or she do?

   _____

   _____

   _____

2. Describe the perfect bedroom that would be *fit for a king*.

   _____

   _____

   _____

3. Describe a person you know who *lives like a king*.

   _____

   _____

   _____

4. List the first six things you would buy if you had a *king's ransom*.

   _____

   _____

   _____

5. Describe a time when you saw *the long arm of the law* in action.

   _____

   _____

   _____

   _____

51626—Go Figure! Exploring Figurative Language

Rulers and Power—Say What? Extensions

Directions: Choose two activities to complete.

> » fall from grace » King's ransom
>
> » fit for a King » live like a king
>
> » the long arm of the law

 ## Figurative and Literal

Choose one figure of speech. Using a sheet of paper folded in half, write "literal" and "figurative" at the top of each side. Under "literal," draw your interpretation of the literal meaning of the figure of speech. Under "figurative," draw your interpretation of the figurative meaning of the figure of speech. Write the figure of speech on the back of your paper.

 ## Conversation Starter

Create a dialogue between you and a friend using at least three figures of speech. Write down your conversation.

 ## Actor's Studio

In a small group, brainstorm five additional figures of speech. Write this week's figures of speech and the five additional figures of speech on small slips of paper. Then, divide into two teams and play a short game of charades using the figures of speech as the secret phrases.

a man's home is his castle

Figures of Speech

» circle the wagons

» come full circle

» you can't fit a square peg in a round hole

» go around in circles

» knock into shape

Overview

Students will enjoy learning about geometry-related figures of speech through the activities in this section. For detailed instructions on how to implement the activities in this lesson, see pages 8–10.

Materials

> copies of *Geometry—Match That Figure!* (page 73)

> copies of *Geometry—Would You Rather?* (page 74)

> copies of *Geometry—Meaningful Words* (page 75)

> copies of *Geometry—Wacky Writing* (page 76)

> copies of *Geometry—Say What? Extensions* (page 77)

> scissors and glue

Additional Figures of Speech

> shipshape

> whip into shape

> square shoulders

> be there or be square

> ideas that don't square

Answer Key

Match That Figure! (page 73)

1. trying to make something work that just isn't going to work

2. to take a defensive position and protect a person or cause

3. returning to the same position you originally had, often with more knowledge or experience

4. improve the condition of something or someone's behavior

5. to spend time trying to do something without making any progress

Pictures will vary but should show an understanding for each figure of speech.

Would You Rather? (page 74)

Check sentences to be sure students' explanations answer the questions.

Meaningful Words (page 75)

1. B   2. A   3. C
Challenge: Check sentences to be sure contexts match the definitions chosen.
4. C   5. B   6. A
Challenge: Check sentences to be sure contexts match the definitions chosen.

Wacky Writing (page 76)

Students' responses should accurately answer each prompt and demonstrate understanding of the figurative phrase.

Say What? Extensions (page 77)

Check to see that students have completed two of the three activities.

Geometry—Match That Figure!

Directions: Cut apart the definition cards. Glue each definition next to the correct phrase. Then, draw a picture to represent each figurative phrase.

Figures of speech	Definitions	Pictures
1. you can't fit a square peg into a round hole (proverb)		
2. circle the wagons (idiom)		
3. come full circle (idiom)		
4. knock into shape (idiom)		
5. go around in circles (idiom)		

| to spend time trying to do something without making any progress | returning to the same position you originally had, often with more knowledge or experience | improve the condition of something or someone's behavior | trying to make something work that just isn't going to work | to take a defensive position and protect a person or cause |

51626—Go Figure! Exploring Figurative Language

Geometry—Would You Rather?

Directions: Read and answer each question.

1. If you were out of shape, what would be a good way to *knock yourself into shape*?

   _____

   _____

   _____

2. Would you rather *circle the wagons* for a bully or someone being bullied? Why?

   _____

   _____

   _____

3. Would you rather *come full circle* and finish a novel you wrote or a game you invented? Why?

   _____

   _____

   _____

4. Would you rather *go around in circles* about what to eat or have someone tell you what to eat? Why?

   _____

   _____

   _____

5. Write your own question using the phrase *you can't fit a square peg into a round hole*.

   _____

   _____

   _____

Geometry—Meaningful Words

Directions: For each sentence, write the letter of the correct definition. Then, create your own sentence using the selected word.

you can't fit a <u>square</u> peg into a round hole	**A.** square (noun): a quadrilateral with four equal sides
	B. square (noun): an open area or plaza in a city
	C. square (adjective): not adventurous; conventional

____ 1. The town square was buzzing with excitement as the townspeople waited for the big announcement.

____ 2. The square room was perfect to make into an office.

____ 3. John's classmates thought he was square because he did not like playing sports.

Challenge: Choose a definition, and write a sentence using the word *square*.

_____

_____

_____

Knock into <u>shape</u>	**A.** shape (noun): the outline of an object
	B. shape (verb): to give definition or form to an object
	C. shape (noun): physically strong and healthy

____ 4. Maria wanted to be in shape for the basketball game, so she trained harder.

____ 5. The children had to shape the clay into their favorite animals.

____ 6. A large crowd came to see the debut of the new car and its unique shape.

Challenge: Choose a definition, and write a sentence using the word *shape*.

_____

_____

_____

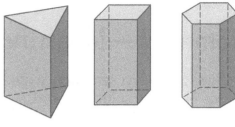

Geometry—Wacky Writing

Directions: Read and answer each prompt.

1. Describe a time when you *came full circle* on your opinion about something.

   _____

   _____

   _____

2. Share a time you *circled the wagons* for a friend in need.

   _____

   _____

   _____

3. Detail a time you tried to make something work despite knowing *you can't fit a square peg into a round hole.*

   _____

   _____

   _____

4. Share a piece of advice you gave to a friend or family member about a problem and how it helped *knock him or her into shape.*

   _____

   _____

   _____

5. Describe a time you had to *go around in circles* about something but then finally got your way.

   _____

   _____

   _____

Geometry—Say What? Extensions

Directions: Choose two activities to complete.

> » circle the wagons » go around in circles
>
> » come full circle » Knock into shape
>
> » you can't fit a square peg in a round hole

✗✓ Example and Non-Example

Choose one figure of speech. Then, write two sentences using the figure of speech appropriately and two using the figure of speech incorrectly. Read the four sentences to a partner and have him or her figure out which two sentences are good examples and which two sentences are non-examples.

Comic Strip

Create a short four- to six-frame comic strip with sketches or simple pictures. Show the humor of one character using a figure of speech and the other character taking it literally.

💬 Conversation Starter

Create a dialogue between you and a friend using at least three figures of speech. Write down your conversation.

go around in circles

Figures of Speech

» add fuel to the fire

» it doesn't add up

» divide and conquer

» look out for number one

» there is safety in numbers

Overview

Students will enjoy learning about number-related figures of speech through the activities in this section. For detailed instructions on how to implement the activities in this lesson, see pages 8–10.

Materials

> copies of *Numbers—Match That Figure!* (page 79)
> copies of *Numbers—Would You Rather?* (page 80)
> copies of *Numbers—Meaningful Words* (page 81)
> copies of *Numbers—Wacky Writing* (page 82)
> copies of *Numbers—Say What? Extensions* (page 83)
> scissors and glue

Additional Figures of Speech

> add insult to injury
> multiply by something
> your days are numbered
> do a number on someone
> public enemy number one
> two's company, three's a crowd

Answer Key

Match That Figure! (page 79)

1. a group of people has more power than one person alone

2. splitting a large task into smaller, more manageable parts

3. a story doesn't make sense based on the facts

4. doing something to make a problem worse

5. take care of your own needs and not the needs of others

Pictures will vary but should show an understanding for each figure of speech.

Would You Rather? (page 80)

Check sentences to be sure students' explanations answer the questions.

Meaningful Words (page 81)

1. A   2. A   3. B
Challenge: Check sentences to be sure contexts match the definitions chosen.
4. A   5. B   6. A
Challenge: Check sentences to be sure contexts match the definitions chosen.

Wacky Writing (page 82)

Students' responses should accurately answer each prompt and demonstrate understanding of the figurative phrase.

Say What? Extensions (page 83)

Check to see that students have completed two of the three activities.

Numbers—Match That Figure!

Directions: Cut apart the definition cards. Glue each definition next to the correct phrase. Then, draw a picture to represent each figurative phrase.

Figures of speech	Definitions	Pictures
1. there is safety in numbers (proverb)		
2. divide and conquer (idiom)		
3. it doesn't add up (idiom)		
4. add fuel to the fire (idiom)		
5. look out for number one (idiom)		

take care of your own needs and not the needs of others	splitting a large task into smaller, more manageable parts	doing something to make a problem worse	a group of people has more power than one person alone	a story doesn't make sense based on the facts

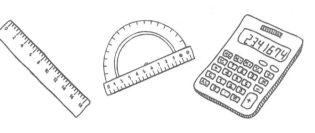

Numbers—Would You Rather?

Directions: Read and answer each question.

1. While discussing a test on which everyone performed poorly, would you rather have *safety in numbers* or meet with the teacher on your own? Why?

   _____

   _____

   _____

2. Would you rather you and your sibling *divide and conquer* the task of cleaning the entire house or doing the family's laundry? Why?

   _____

   _____

   _____

3. Would you rather *look out for number one* and save your money or lend it to a friend in need? Why?

   _____

   _____

   _____

4. Would you rather challenge a classmate whose story *doesn't add up* or just let him or her tell the story that you know is a lie? Why?

   _____

   _____

   _____

5. Write your own question using the phrase *add fuel to the fire*.

   _____

   _____

   _____

Numbers—Meaningful Words

Directions: For each sentence, write the letter of the correct definition.
Then, create your own sentence using the selected word.

<u>divide</u> and conquer	**A.** divide (verb): to separate into parts or groups **B.** divide (noun): a division, usually of opinions

____ 1. The road eventually divided between the route to the city and the route to the country.

____ 2. The kids tried to divide the chores evenly between them.

____ 3. After the new boss was hired, it caused a divide in the company.

Challenge: Choose a definition, and write a sentence using the word *divide*.

_____

_____

_____

add <u>fuel</u> to the fire	**A.** fuel (noun): an energy source for engines or something with power **B.** fuel (verb): something that encourages or stimulates

____ 4. The race cars had to be full of fuel before starting the big contest.

____ 5. Maria had a long day ahead of her, so she fueled up with a healthy breakfast.

____ 6. When the price of fuel increases, it gets expensive to go on a road trip.

Challenge: Choose a definition, and write a sentence using the word *fuel*.

_____

_____

_____

Numbers—Wacky Writing

Directions: Read and answer each prompt.

1. Describe a time when you heard a story that *didn't add up*. Did you say anything?

   _____

   _____

   _____

2. Do you think it is a good idea to *divide and conquer* as the boss of a company? Why or why not?

   _____

   _____

   _____

3. When would it be helpful to have *safety in numbers*?

   _____

   _____

   _____

4. Is it easy to *look out for number one* before looking out for others? Why or why not?

   _____

   _____

   _____

5. Are you the type of person to *add fuel to the fire* when someone is upset? Why or why not?

   _____

   _____

   _____

Numbers—Say What? Extensions

Directions: Choose two activities to complete.

> » add fuel to the fire » it doesn't add up
>
> » divide and conquer » look out for number one
>
> » there is safety in numbers

 ## Actor's Studio

In a small group, brainstorm five additional figures of speech. Write this week's figures of speech and the five additional figures of speech on small slips of paper. Then, divide into two teams and play a short game of charades using the figures of speech as the secret phrases.

 ## Word Association

Choose one word to associate with each figure of speech. Then, find a partner and quiz each other to see who can solve which figures of speech are associated with the words you have chosen. For example, you can choose "storm" if the figure of speech is *it's raining cats and dogs*.

 ## Say It, Don't Spray It!

Work with a small group to write and tell a story that includes all five figures of speech. One person begins the story. Then, each person takes a turn adding an idea to the story. Continue the story until all figures of speech have been used and the story comes to an end.

it doesn't add up

Figures of Speech

» a day late and a dollar short

» a fool and his money are soon parted

» put your money where your mouth is

» phony as a three-dollar bill

» stop on a dime

Overview

Students will enjoy learning about money-related figures of speech through the activities in this section. For detailed instructions on how to implement the activities in this lesson, see pages 8–10.

Materials

> copies of *Money—Match That Figure!* (page 85)
> copies of *Money—Would You Rather?* (page 86)
> copies of *Money—Meaningful Words* (page 87)
> copies of *Money—Wacky Writing* (page 88)
> copies of *Money—Say What? Extensions* (page 89)
> scissors and glue
> index cards

Additional Figures of Speech

> cold hard cash
> a dime a dozen
> cash in your chips
> not worth a dime
> pennies from heaven
> don't take any wooden nickels
> ten-dollar hat on a five-cent head
> nickel and dime someone to death
> don't have two pennies to rub together

Answer Key

Match That Figure! (page 85)

1. an action was done too late or with not enough of what was needed to get a task done

2. to live up to what you say you will do

3. something that is obviously fake

4. if you aren't smart with your money, you will waste it

5. to come to a stop quickly

Pictures will vary but should show an understanding for each figure of speech.

Would You Rather? (page 86)

Check sentences to be sure students' explanations answer the questions.

Meaningful Words (page 87)

1. A   2. B   3. A
Challenge: Check sentences to be sure contexts match the definitions chosen.
4. B   5. A   6. B
Challenge: Check sentences to be sure contexts match the definitions chosen.

Wacky Writing (page 88)

Students' responses should accurately answer each prompt and demonstrate understanding of the figurative phrase.

Say What? Extensions (page 89)

Check to see that students have completed two of the three activities.

Money—Match That Figure!

Directions: Cut apart the definition cards. Glue each definition next to the correct phrase. Then, draw a picture to represent each figurative phrase.

Figures of speech	Definitions	Pictures
1. a day late and a dollar short (idiom)		
2. put your money where your mouth is (idiom)		
3. phony as a three-dollar bill (idiom)		
4. a fool and his money are soon parted (proverb)		
5. stop on a dime (idiom)		

| if you aren't smart with your money, you will waste it | to come to a stop quickly | an action was done too late or with not enough of what was needed to get a task done | something that is obviously fake | to live up to what you say you will do |

Money—Would You Rather?

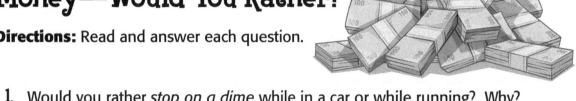

Directions: Read and answer each question.

1. Would you rather *stop on a dime* while in a car or while running? Why?

_____

_____

_____

2. Would you rather write or read a story as *phony as a three-dollar bill?* Why?

_____

_____

_____

3. Would you rather have a friend that *puts his money where his mouth is* or a friend who makes promises that he doesn't always keep? Why?

_____

_____

_____

4. Would you rather avoid being *a day late and a dollar short* when planning to go to an amusement park or a concert? Why?

_____

_____

_____

5. Write your own question using the phrase *a fool and his money are soon parted*.

_____

_____

_____

Money—Meaningful Words

Directions: For each sentence, write the letter of the correct definition. Then, create your own sentence using the selected word.

put your money where your <u>mouth</u> is	**A.** mouth (noun): the opening through which food passes through to the body; the part of the face that includes the lips **B.** mouth (verb): to form words with lips without sound coming out

____ 1. Olivia stood with her mouth agape after the magician completed his impressive trick.

____ 2. Thomas mouthed the words to his favorite song.

____ 3. My mouth started salivating as soon as I smelled the freshly baked cookies.

Challenge: Choose a definition, and write a sentence using the word *mouth*.

_____

_____

a day late and a dollar <u>short</u>	**A.** short (adverb): quick and to the point **B.** short (adjective): not tall in height

____ 4. Everyone thought Marisol was younger than Jon because she was shorter than him.

____ 5. Kara was annoyed, so she was very short with Mark.

____ 6. Angela was dismayed to learn she was too short to get on the roller coaster.

Challenge: Choose a definition, and write a sentence using the word *short*.

_____

_____

Money—Wacky Writing

Directions: Read and answer each prompt.

1. Describe a character in a book or movie that you think is *phony as a three-dollar bill*. Explain why you picked the character.

   _____

   _____

   _____

2. Name a time you frivolously spent money and then realized *a fool and his or her money are soon parted*.

   _____

   _____

   _____

3. In which sport do you think players have to *stop on a dime* the most often? Why?

   _____

   _____

   _____

4. Describe a time you were *a day late and a dollar short* and missed out on doing something you really wanted to do.

   _____

   _____

   _____

5. Name someone who often doesn't *put his or her money where his or her mouth is*. Do you have respect for this person? Why or why not?

   _____

   _____

   _____

Money—Say What? Extensions

Directions: Choose two activities to complete.

> » a fool and his money are soon parted » phony as a three-dollar bill
>
> » a day late and a dollar short » stop on a dime
>
> » put your money where your mouth is

 Matching Game

Create a matching game with a partner. Using 10 index cards, write each figure of speech on one card and your own definition for each phrase on another card. Mix up all the cards. Time how long it takes you to match each figure of speech with its definition. Have your partner try to beat your time. Each person goes twice to see who can achieve the fastest time.

 Short Story

Write a short description of something that recently happened to you using two of the figures of speech. Be sure the figures of speech are used correctly. Underline them when you are finished.

👓 **Read All About It!**

With a partner, pretend you work for a news organization and have to write one paragraph about something that happened in your town. The story should contain at least two of this week's figures of speech.

put your money
where your mouth is

51626—Go Figure! Exploring Figurative Language **89**

Figures of Speech

» all in good time

» a stitch in time saves nine

» time to kill

» make up for lost time

» procrastination is the thief of time

Overview

Students will enjoy learning about time-related figures of speech through the activities in this section. For detailed instructions on how to implement the activities in this lesson, see pages 8–10.

Materials

> copies of *Time—Match That Figure!* (page 91)
> copies of *Time—Would You Rather?* (page 92)
> copies of *Time—Meaningful Words* (page 93)
> copies of *Time—Wacky Writing* (page 94)
> copies of *Time—Say What? Extensions* (page 95)
> scissors and glue
> index cards

Additional Figures of Speech

> time out
> crunch time
> eleventh hour
> devil of a time
> at the last minute
> time on one's hands
> only a matter of time
> keeping banker's hours
> the darkest hour is just before dawn

Answer Key

Match That Figure! (page 91)

1. if you fix a small problem right away, it will not become a bigger problem later

2. be patient because things will happen when they are supposed to happen

3. to have to find something unimportant to do while you are waiting for time to pass

4. to catch up after missing something, or a period of slow going

5. if you put off doing what you need to do, you will run out of time

Pictures will vary but should show an understanding for each figure of speech.

Would You Rather? (page 92)

Check sentences to be sure students' explanations answer the questions.

Meaningful Words (page 93)

1. A   2. A   3. B

Challenge: Check sentences to be sure contexts match the definitions chosen.

4. B   5. A   6. C

Challenge: Check sentences to be sure contexts match the definitions chosen.

Wacky Writing (page 94)

Students' responses should accurately answer each prompt and demonstrate understanding of the figurative phrase.

Say What? Extensions (page 95)

Check to see that students have completed two of the three activities.

Time—Match That Figure!

Directions: Cut apart the definition cards. Glue each definition next to the correct phrase. Then, draw a picture to represent each figurative phrase.

Figures of speech	Definitions	Pictures
1. a stitch in time saves nine (proverb)		
2. all in good time (idiom)		
3. time to kill (idiom)		
4. make up for lost time (idiom)		
5. procrastination is the thief of time (proverb)		

to catch up after missing something, or a period of slow going	if you put off doing what you need to do, you will run out of time	if you fix a small problem right away, it will not become a bigger problem later	be patient because things will happen when they are supposed to happen	to have to find something unimportant to do while you are waiting for time to pass

Time—Would You Rather?

Directions: Read and answer each question.

1. Would you rather have *time to kill* at a park or a library? Why?

   _____
   _____
   _____

2. If things happen *all in good time*, would you rather wait six months for the new version of a smartphone, or get the current version now? Why?

   _____
   _____
   _____

3. Considering a *stitch in time saves nine*, would you rather finish your homework the day it's assigned or ignore it until the night before the deadline?

   _____
   _____
   _____

4. Since *procrastination is the thief of time*, would you rather put off chores or your homework? Why?

   _____
   _____
   _____

5. Write your own question using the phrase *make up for lost time*.

   _____
   _____
   _____

Time—Meaningful Words

Directions: For each sentence, write the letter of the correct definition. Then, create your own sentence using the selected word.

| make up for <u>lost</u> time | **A.** lost (adjective): an object not able to be found or a person who can't find where they are going |
| | **B.** lost (adjective): unable to figure something out |

____ 1. We finally found my dad's lost keys in the freezer!

____ 2. Clarissa purchased a navigation system for her car because she gets lost easily.

____ 3. Pedro became lost while working on his algebra homework and decided to call a friend for help.

Challenge: Choose a definition, and write a sentence using the word *lost*.

_____

_____

_____

<u>time</u> to kill	**A.** time (noun): a limited period or interval
	B. time (noun): the measure of a part of the day or night
	C. time (verb): to measure or record speed

____ 4. "Excuse me, do you have the time?" Gerald asked.

____ 5. We all showed up at the ice-skating rink around the same time.

____ 6. The coach used a stopwatch to time the runners during their race.

Challenge: Choose a definition, and write a sentence using the word *time*.

_____

_____

_____

Time—Wacky Writing

Directions: Read and answer each prompt.

1. Describe an occasion when you needed to *make up for lost time* with a friend.

   _____

   _____

   _____

2. How did you keep yourself occupied the last time you had *time to kill*?

   _____

   _____

   _____

3. Share when *procrastination was the thief of time* and you missed something fun because you had wasted your time.

   _____

   _____

   _____

4. What is something you hope will happen *all in good time* for you?

   _____

   _____

   _____

5. Write about an instance when you learned that *a stitch in time saves nine*.

   _____

   _____

   _____

Time—Say What? Extensions

Directions: Choose two activities to complete.

> » all in good time » a stitch in time saves nine
>
> » time to kill » make up for lost time
>
> » procrastination is the thief of time

 ## Memory Game

Using 10 index cards, write each figure of speech and each definition on a separate card. Then, turn them over and play a quick memory game with a partner. Play twice to see who can get the most overall matches between the games.

 ## Poetry Time

Choose one of the figures of speech. Then, create a short poem or rap with eight lines that would help someone younger than you understand the meaning of the figure of speech. You can use the definition, examples, and your own creativity to make it fun and interesting.

 ## Mime Time

Take turns acting out all five of the figures of speech with your partner or group members. You may only act out the clues with body language and gestures. You may not use your voice!

a stitch in time saves nine

Figures of Speech

» beyond measure » the meter is running

» go the extra mile » whole nine yards

» if you give someone an inch, he or she will take a mile

Overview

Students will enjoy learning about measurement-related figures of speech through the activities in this section. For detailed instructions on how to implement the activities in this lesson, see pages 8–10.

Materials

> copies of *Measurement—Match That Figure!* (page 97)

> copies of *Measurement—Would You Rather?* (page 98)

> copies of *Measurement—Meaningful Words* (page 99)

> copies of *Measurement—Wacky Writing* (page 100)

> copies of *Measurement—Say What? Extensions* (page 101)

> scissors and glue

Additional Figures of Speech

> inch along

> inch by inch

> for good measure

> talk a mile a minute

> a million miles away

> measure up to someone

> all wool and a yard wide

> within an inch of one's life

Answer Key

Match That Figure! (page 97)

1. if you allow someone to have a little of something, the person will take a lot more

2. put forth extra effort to go above and beyond what is expected

3. something to an extreme degree, sometimes more than can be quantified

4. the entire amount; doing everything for someone

5. cost and consequences are increasing while waiting for a decision

Pictures will vary but should show an understanding for each figure of speech.

Would You Rather? (page 98)

Check sentences to be sure students' explanations answer the questions.

Meaningful Words (page 99)

1. C   2. B   3. A
Challenge: Check sentences to be sure contexts match the definitions chosen.
4. B   5. A   6. C
Challenge: Check sentences to be sure contexts match the definitions chosen.

Wacky Writing (page 100)

Students' responses should accurately answer each prompt and demonstrate understanding of the figurative phrase.

Say What? Extensions (page 101)

Check to see that students have completed two of the three activities.

Measurement—Match That Figure!

Directions: Cut apart the definition cards. Glue each definition next to the correct phrase. Then, draw a picture to represent each figurative phrase.

Figures of speech	Definitions	Pictures
1. if you give someone an inch, he or she will take a mile (proverb)		
2. go the extra mile (idiom)		
3. beyond measure (idiom)		
4. whole nine yards (idiom)		
5. the meter is running (idiom)		

put forth extra effort to go above and beyond what is expected	if you allow someone to have a little of something, the person will take more	cost and consequences are increasing while waiting for a decision	something to an extreme degree, sometimes more than can be quantified	the entire amount; doing everything for someone

Measurement—Would You Rather?

Directions: Read and answer each question.

1. Would you rather have help putting together a party or be in charge of the *whole nine yards* yourself? Why?

   _____

   _____

   _____

2. Would you rather have love or money *beyond measure*? Why?

   _____

   _____

   _____

3. Would you rather *go the extra mile* when completing a task for yourself or for others? Why?

   _____

   _____

   _____

4. Would you rather have *the meter running* for a timed math test or a reading test? Why?

   _____

   _____

   _____

5. Write your own question using the phrase *if you give someone an inch, he or she will take a mile*.

   _____

   _____

   _____

Measurement—Meaningful Words

Directions: For each sentence, write the letter of the correct definition. Then, create your own sentence using the selected word.

whole nine <u>yards</u>	**A.** yard (noun): a unit of measurement
	B. yard (noun): the ground surrounding a house
	C. yard (noun): an enclosure for a specific purpose or business

____ 1. The old junkyard had many hidden treasures in it.

____ 2. Gary loved to play in his backyard and pretend he was on a treasure hunt.

____ 3. Lindsay's favorite race was the 100-yard dash.

Challenge: Choose a definition, and write a sentence using the word *yards*.

_____

_____

the <u>meter</u> is running	**A.** meter (noun): a unit of measurement in the metric system
	B. meter (noun): a rhythmic element relating to beats in music or flow in poetry
	C. meter (noun): an instrument used for measuring amounts of something used

____ 4. The meter of the song caused the audience to start clapping to the beat.

____ 5. Ed won the egg drop competition when his egg survived the 100-meter drop.

____ 6. Lucy put coins in the parking meter to avoid receiving a parking ticket.

Challenge: Choose a definition, and write a sentence using the word *meter*.

_____

_____

Measurement—Wacky Writing

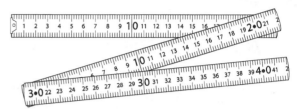

Directions: Read and answer each prompt.

1. Describe a time when *the meter was running* and you had to make a decision quickly.

   _____

   _____

   _____

2. Share a time when you decided to *go the extra mile* and someone was very appreciative of your efforts.

   _____

   _____

   _____

3. Describe your dream party in which a party planner would go the *whole nine yards*.

   _____

   _____

   _____

4. Explain why it's smart to speak up when you disagree with a decision because, if you *give someone an inch, he or she will take a mile*.

   _____

   _____

   _____

5. Describe something that someone has done for you that was *beyond measure*.

   _____

   _____

   _____

Measurement—Say What? Extensions

Directions: Choose two activities to complete.

> » beyond measure　　» the meter is running
>
> » go the extra mile　　» whole nine yards
>
> » if you give someone an inch, he or she will take a mile

 ### The Extra Mile

With a partner, write a list of 10 things you could do to *go the extra mile* at home. Then, underline your favorite one. Try to do the underlined task at home within 24 hours.

 ### Figurative and Literal

Choose one figure of speech. Using a sheet of paper folded in half, write "literal" and "figurative" at the top of each side. Under "literal," draw your interpretation of the literal meaning of the figure of speech. Under "figurative," draw your interpretation of the figurative meaning of the figure of speech. Write the figure of speech on the back of your paper.

 ### Tell Me a Tale

Create a fairy tale with a small group. The story should be funny, short, and use at least two figures of speech. Each person can only say one word at a time to tell the story. For example, the first person might say "once." Then, the next person would say "upon." The third person would say "a," and the fourth person would say "time."

the meter is running

Figures of Speech

» get the ball rolling

» off to a flying start

» never in a million years

» ring in the new year

» year in, year out

Overview

Students will enjoy learning about New Year's Day-related figures of speech through the activities in this section. For detailed instructions on how to implement the activities in this lesson, see pages 8–10.

Materials

> copies of *New Year's Day—Match That Figure!* (page 103)

> copies of *New Year's Day—Would You Rather?* (page 104)

> copies of *New Year's Day—Meaningful Words* (page 105)

> copies of *New Year's Day—Wacky Writing* (page 106)

> copies of *New Year's Day—Say What? Extensions* (page 107)

> scissors and glue

Additional Figures of Speech

> false start

> fresh start

> jump start

> year in, year out

> getting on in years

> move the goalposts

> light years away from

> fall short of your goal

Answer Key

Match That Figure! (page 103)

1. celebrating the new year

2. doing something repeatedly or all the time

3. starting a task with a lot of success

4. not wanting to ever do or agree to something

5. to get a process or activity started

Pictures will vary but should show an understanding for each figure of speech.

Would You Rather? (page 104)

Check sentences to be sure students' explanations answer the questions.

Meaningful Words (page 105)

1. C   2. B   3. A

Challenge: Check sentences to be sure contexts match the definitions chosen.

4. A   5. B   6. A

Challenge: Check sentences to be sure contexts match the definitions chosen.

Wacky Writing (page 106)

Students' responses should accurately answer each prompt and demonstrate understanding of the figurative phrase.

Say What? Extensions (page 107)

Check to see that students have completed two of the three activities.

New Year's Day—Match That Figure!

Directions: Cut apart the definition cards. Glue each definition next to the correct phrase. Then, draw a picture to represent each figurative phrase.

Figures of speech	Definitions	Pictures
1. ring in the new year (idiom)		
2. year in, year out (idiom)		
3. off to a flying start (idiom)		
4. never in a million years (idiom)		
5. get the ball rolling (idiom)		

doing something repeatedly or all the time	starting a task with a lot of success	not wanting to ever do or agree to something	to get a process or activity started	celebrating the new year

51626—Go Figure! Exploring Figurative Language

New Year's Day—Would You Rather?

Directions: Read and answer each question.

1. Would you rather be *off to a flying start* on a project and finish on time or have a slow start and finish early? Why?

   _____

   _____

   _____

2. Would you rather skydive with a friend or choose to *never do this in a million years*? Why?

   _____

   _____

   _____

3. Would you rather *ring in the new year* at a party at your house or someone else's house? Why?

   _____

   _____

   _____

4. Would you rather have snow or sun *year in, year out*? Why?

   _____

   _____

   _____

5. Write your own question using the phrase *get the ball rolling*.

   _____

   _____

   _____

New Year's Day—Meaningful Words

Directions: For each sentence, write the letter of the correct definition. Then, create your own sentence using the selected word.

ring in the new year	**A.** ring (noun): a band of precious metal worn on a finger
	B. ring (noun): an object of circular shape
	C. ring (verb): to cause a sound from a bell or other instrument

____ 1. The children were excited to hear the bell ring on the last day of school.

____ 2. The fancy dinner table setting included glasses, utensils, and decorative napkin rings.

____ 3. The woman was upset when she realized she lost her wedding ring while swimming.

Challenge: Choose a definition, and write a sentence using the word *ring*.

_____

_____

| get the ball rolling | **A.** ball (noun): a sphere-shaped object, often used for playing sports |
| | **B.** ball (noun): a large, formal party, often with dancing |

____ 4. Terri kicked the ball so hard that it went over the fence!

____ 5. Hundreds of people were invited to the charity ball.

____ 6. Keisha passed the ball to her teammate during the game.

Challenge: Choose a definition, and write a sentence using the word *ball*.

_____

_____

New Year's Day—Wacky Writing

Directions: Read and answer each prompt.

1. Describe your favorite way to *ring in the new year*.

   _____

   _____

   _____

2. Name three things you would *never do in a million years*.

   _____

   _____

   _____

3. Describe something that would help motivate your classmates to *get the ball rolling* when you are working on a group project.

   _____

   _____

   _____

4. In business, describe why it would be good to *get off to a flying start* if you had a big order come in or a project that needed to be done quickly.

   _____

   _____

   _____

5. Describe something your parents make you do *year in, year out*, whether you want to or not.

   _____

   _____

   _____

New Year's Day—Say What? Extensions

Directions: Choose two activities to complete.

> » get the ball rolling
>
> » never in a million years
>
> » year in, year out
>
> » off to a flying start
>
> » ring in the new year

 ### Poetry Time

Choose one of the figures of speech. Then, create a short poem or rap with eight lines that would help someone younger than you understand the meaning of the figure of speech. You can use the definition, examples, and your own creativity to make it fun and interesting.

 ### Tell Me a Tale

Create a fairy tale with a small group. The story should be funny, short, and use at least two figures of speech. Each person can only say one word at a time to tell the story. For example, the first person might say "once." Then, the next person would say "upon." The third person would say "a," and the fourth person would say "time."

 ### Figurative and Literal

Choose one figure of speech. Using a sheet of paper folded in half, write "literal" and "figurative" at the top of each side. Under "literal," draw your interpretation of the literal meaning of the figure of speech. Under "figurative," draw your interpretation of the figurative meaning of the figure of speech. Write the figure of speech on the back of your paper.

get the ball rolling

Figures of Speech

» eat your heart out

» heart in your mouth

» take something to heart

» wear your heart on your sleeve

» absence makes the heart grow fonder

Overview

Students will enjoy learning about Valentine's Day-related figures of speech through the activities in this section. For detailed instructions on how to implement the activities in this lesson, see pages 8–10.

Materials

> copies of *Valentine's Day—Match That Figure!* (page 109)

> copies of *Valentine's Day—Would You Rather?* (page 110)

> copies of *Valentine's Day—Meaningful Words* (page 111)

> copies of *Valentine's Day—Wacky Writing* (page 112)

> copies of *Valentine's Day—Say What? Extensions* (page 113)

> scissors and glue

Additional Figures of Speech

> bless your heart

> change of heart

> have a heart

> cry your heart out

> set your heart at rest

> have your heart set on

> from the bottom of your heart

> cross your heart and hope to die

> cold-hearted, soft-hearted, big-hearted

Answer Key

Match That Figure! (page 109)

1. to display one's feelings openly

2. being anxious or scared about something

3. when you are away from someone special, you miss him or her

4. to be jealous or envious of something

5. to understand deeply what someone has told you

Pictures will vary but should show an understanding for each figure of speech.

Would You Rather? (page 110)

Check sentences to be sure students' explanations answer the questions.

Meaningful Words (page 111)

1. B   2. A   3. B

Challenge: Check sentences to be sure contexts match the definitions chosen.

4. B   5. B   6. A

Challenge: Check sentences to be sure contexts match the definitions chosen.

Wacky Writing (page 112)

Students' responses should accurately answer each prompt and demonstrate understanding of the figurative phrase.

Say What? Extensions (page 113)

Check to see that students have completed two of the three activities.

Valentine's Day—Match That Figure!

Directions: Cut apart the definition cards. Glue each definition next to the correct phrase. Then, draw a picture to represent each figurative phrase.

Figures of speech	Definitions	Pictures
1. wear your heart on your sleeve (idiom)		
2. heart in your mouth (idiom)		
3. absence makes the heart grow fonder (proverb)		
4. eat your heart out (idiom)		
5. take something to heart (idiom)		

to display one's feelings openly	to be jealous or envious of something	to understand deeply what someone has told you	being anxious or scared about something	when you are away from someone special, you miss him or her

Valentine's Day—Would You Rather?

Directions: Read and answer each question.

1. Would you rather tell someone to *eat his or her heart out* once you proved the person wrong or just know you did a good job without telling him or her? Why?

   _____

   _____

   _____

2. Would you rather have your *heart in your mouth* in a haunted house or while watching a scary movie? Why?

   _____

   _____

   _____

3. Would you rather *wear your heart on your sleeve* or rarely show your emotions? Why?

   _____

   _____

   _____

4. If *absence makes the heart grow fonder*, would you rather not see your best friend for a week or not watch television for a week? Why?

   _____

   _____

   _____

5. Write your own question using the phrase *take something to heart.*

   _____

   _____

   _____

Valentine's Day—Meaningful Words

i ♥ you

Directions: For each sentence, write the letter of the correct definition.
Then, create your own sentence using the selected word.

| <u>wear</u> your heart on your sleeve | **A.** wear (verb): to put on the body as clothing |
| | **B.** wear (verb): to deteriorate or be used up over time |

____ 1. Jocelyn liked to wear out her jeans so they had a distressed look.

____ 2. Linda wanted to wear her new outfit to her job interview on Saturday.

____ 3. Josh tried not to wear down the eraser on his pencil while drawing in art class.

Challenge: Choose a definition, and write a sentence using the word *wear*.

_____

_____

_____

| eat your <u>heart</u> out | **A.** heart (noun): an organ in the body that circulates blood |
| | **B.** heart (noun): the center of emotion |

____ 4. Her heart told her to stand up for her beliefs.

____ 5. Our teacher said the surprise birthday gift we purchased brought joy to her heart.

____ 6. Dr. Phillips used his stethoscope to listen to the newborn baby's heartbeat.

Challenge: Choose a definition, and write a sentence using the word *heart*.

_____

_____

_____

Valentine's Day—Wacky Writing

Directions: Read and answer each prompt.

1. What makes you so nervous you feel as though your *heart is in your mouth*?

   _____

   _____

   _____

2. Since *absence makes the heart grow fonder*, name two people that you would miss the most if they went away for a month. Why did you choose them?

   _____

   _____

   _____

3. List three people whose advice you would *take to heart*.

   _____

   _____

   _____

4. Are you someone who is likely to *wear your heart on your sleeve*? Why or why not?

   _____

   _____

   _____

5. Describe a time when you did something that others thought you couldn't do and you wanted to tell them to *eat their hearts out!*

   _____

   _____

   _____

Valentine's Day—Say What? Extensions

Directions: Choose two activities to complete.

> » eat your heart out   » take something to heart
>
> » heart in your mouth   » wear your heart on your sleeve
>
> » absence makes the heart grow fonder

 ### Word Association

Choose one word to associate with each figure of speech. Then, find a partner and quiz each other to see who can solve which figures of speech are associated with the words you have chosen. For example, you can choose "storm" if the figure of speech is *it's raining cats and dogs*.

 ### Valentine's Day Card

Pick a famous couple from literature or history. Create a Valentine's Day card from one person to the other that uses all the figures of speech.

 ### Conversation Starter

Create a dialogue between you and a friend using at least three figures of speech. Write down your conversation.

wear your heart on your sleeve

Figures of Speech

» beginner's luck » don't press your luck

» heart of gold » march to the beat of your own drum

» pot of gold at the end of the rainbow

Overview

Students will enjoy learning about St. Patrick's Day-related figures of speech through the activities in this section. For detailed instructions on how to implement the activities in this lesson, see pages 8–10.

Materials

> copies of *St. Patrick's Day—Match That Figure!* (page 115)

> copies of *St. Patrick's Day—Would You Rather?* (page 116)

> copies of *St. Patrick's Day—Meaningful Words* (page 117)

> copies of *St. Patrick's Day—Wacky Writing* (page 118)

> copies of *St. Patrick's Day—Say What? Extensions* (page 119)

> scissors and glue

> index cards

Additional Figures of Speech

> tough luck

> lucky streak

> luck of the draw

> luck of the Irish

> streak of bad luck

> down on your luck

> stroke of good luck

> more luck than sense

Answer Key

Match That Figure! (page 115)

1. to be very generous, sincere, and friendly

2. don't risk good fortune by being greedy and trying to get more

3. getting a reward at the end of a journey or difficult task

4. to do your own thing and not follow what everyone else is doing

5. being good at something challenging the first time you try it

Pictures will vary but should show an understanding for each figure of speech.

Would You Rather? (page 116)

Check sentences to be sure students' explanations answer the questions.

Meaningful Words (page 117)

1. A 2. C 3. B

Challenge: Check sentences to be sure contexts match the definitions chosen.

4. B 5. A 6. B

Challenge: Check sentences to be sure contexts match the definitions chosen.

Wacky Writing (page 118)

Students' responses should accurately answer each prompt and demonstrate understanding of the figurative phrase.

Say What? Extensions (page 119)

Check to see that students have completed two of the three activities.

St. Patrick's Day—Match That Figure!

Directions: Cut apart the definition cards. Glue each definition next to the correct phrase. Then, draw a picture to represent each figurative phrase.

Figures of speech	Definitions	Pictures
1. heart of gold (idiom)		
2. don't press your luck (idiom)		
3. pot of gold at the end of the rainbow (idiom)		
4. march to the beat of your own drum (proverb)		
5. beginner's luck (idiom)		

being good at something challenging the first time you try it	getting a reward at the end of a journey or difficult task	to be very generous, sincere, and friendly	don't risk good fortune by being greedy and trying to get more	to do your own thing and not follow what everyone else is doing

St. Patrick's Day—Would You Rather?

Directions: Read and answer each question.

1. Would you rather rely on *beginner's luck* or practice when learning a new skill?

   _____

   _____

   _____

2. Would you rather have a *heart of gold* or a piece of real gold jewelry? Why?

   _____

   _____

   _____

3. Would you rather follow what's popular or *march to the beat of your own drum*? Why?

   _____

   _____

   _____

4. Would you rather *press your luck* in a game or play it safe and stop while you are ahead? Why?

   _____

   _____

   _____

5. Write your own question using the phrase *pot of gold at the end of the rainbow.*

   _____

   _____

   _____

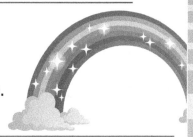

St. Patrick's Day—Meaningful Words

Directions: For each sentence, write the letter of the correct definition. Then, create your own sentence using the selected word.

<u>march</u> to the beat of your own drum	**A.** march (verb): to walk in a steady and organized way, sometimes in groups
	B. march (noun): a sometimes long or exhaustive walk, often for a cause or charity
	C. march (verb): to move on in time

____ 1. The band learned how to play their instruments and march at the same time.

____ 2. Even though we have challenges, time marches on.

____ 3. The group's march was to help raise money for cancer research.

Challenge: Choose a definition, and write a sentence using the word *march*.

_____

_____

| heart of <u>gold</u> | **A.** gold (noun): a precious metallic element |
| | **B.** gold (adjective): a bright yellowish color |

____ 4. I painted the sun a shade of gold amid the sunset.

____ 5. Juan gave his wife 14-carat gold earrings for their anniversary.

____ 6. Marsha picked out a gold top to wear to the concert.

Challenge: Choose a definition, and write a sentence using the word *gold*.

_____

_____

St. Patrick's Day—Wacky Writing

Directions: Read and answer each prompt.

1. Explain a situation when you warned a friend not to *press his or her luck*.

   _____

   _____

   _____

2. Name two people you know who have *hearts of gold*. Explain why you picked them.

   _____

   _____

   _____

3. Describe a time when you *marched to the beat of your own drum* even though it may have been uncomfortable.

   _____

   _____

   _____

4. Describe a time when you worked hard for something and there was a *pot of gold at the end of the rainbow*.

   _____

   _____

   _____

5. Describe a time you had *beginner's luck*.

   _____

   _____

   _____

51626—Go Figure! Exploring Figurative Language

St. Patrick's Day—Say What? Extensions

Directions: Choose two activities to complete.

> » beginner's luck » don't press your luck
>
> » heart of gold » pot of gold at the end of the rainbow
>
> » march to the beat of your own drum

 Example and Non-Example

Choose one figure of speech. Then, write two sentences using the figure of speech appropriately and two using the figure of speech incorrectly. Read the four sentences to a partner and have him or her figure out which two sentences are good examples and which two sentences are non-examples.

 Matching Game

Create a matching game with a partner. Using 10 index cards, write each figure of speech on one card and your own definition for each phrase on another card. Mix up all the cards. Time how long it takes you to match each figure of speech with its definition. Have your partner try to beat your time. Each person goes twice to see who can achieve the fastest time.

 Mime Time

Take turns acting out all five of the figures of speech with your partner or group members. You may only act out the clues with body language and gestures. You may not use your voice!

pot of gold at the end of the rainbow

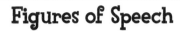

Figures of Speech

» aim for the stars

» a red flag

» wave the white flag

» change your stripes

» stars in one's eyes

Overview

Students will enjoy learning about patriotic-related figures of speech through the activities in this section. For detailed instructions on how to implement the activities in this lesson, see pages 8–10.

Materials

> copies of *Patriotic Days: Stars and Stripes—Match That Figure!* (page 121)

> copies of *Patriotic Days: Stars and Stripes—Would You Rather?* (page 122)

> copies of *Patriotic Days: Stars and Stripes—Meaningful Words* (page 123)

> copies of *Patriotic Days: Stars and Stripes—Wacky Writing* (page 124)

> copies of *Patriotic Days: Stars and Stripes—Say What? Extensions* (page 125)

> scissors and glue

Additional Figures of Speech

> American dream

> earn your stripes

> put the flags out

> flag someone down

> second-class citizen

> American as apple pie

Answer Key

Match That Figure! (page 121)

1. set your goals high

2. a change in your opinion or allegiance to something

3. expecting something great to happen

4. signaling that you want to give up, make a truce, or make peace

5. a sign of something that could be trouble or a problem down the road

Pictures will vary but should show an understanding for each figure of speech.

Would You Rather? (page 122)

Check sentences to be sure students' explanations answer the questions.

Meaningful Words (page 123)

1. B   2. A   3. C
Challenge: Check sentences to be sure contexts match the definitions chosen.
4. C   5. B   6. A
Challenge: Check sentences to be sure contexts match the definitions chosen.

Wacky Writing (page 124)

Students' responses should accurately answer each prompt and demonstrate understanding of the figurative phrase.

Say What? Extensions (page 125)

Check to see that students have completed two of the three activities.

Patriotic Days: Stars and Stripes—Match That Figure!

Directions: Cut apart the definition cards. Glue each definition next to the correct phrase. Then, draw a picture to represent each figurative phrase.

Figures of speech	Definitions	Pictures
1. aim for the stars (idiom)		
2. change your stripes (idiom)		
3. stars in one's eyes (idiom)		
4. wave the white flag (idiom)		
5. a red flag (idiom)		

| a change in your opinion or allegiance to something | signaling that you want to give up, make a truce, or make peace | a sign of something that could be trouble or a problem down the road | expecting something great to happen | set your goals high |

51626—Go Figure! Exploring Figurative Language

Patriotic Days: Stars and Stripes—Would You Rather?

Directions: Read and answer each question.

1. Would you rather have *stars in your eyes* when meeting a famous singer or an athlete? Why?

   _____

   _____

   _____

2. Would you rather *aim for the stars* and miss, or set realistic goals and always achieve them? Why?

   _____

   _____

   _____

3. Would you rather be the one *to wave the white flag* in an argument or wait for your opponent to give in? Why?

   _____

   _____

   _____

4. Would you rather *change your stripes* and admit you are wrong or keep defending your position to save face? Why?

   _____

   _____

   _____

5. Write your own question using the phrase *a red flag*.

   _____

   _____

   _____

Patriotic Days: Stars and Stripes—Meaningful Words

Directions: For each sentence, write the letter of the correct definition. Then, create your own sentence using the selected word.

aim for the <u>stars</u>	**A.** star (noun): a self-luminous heavenly body **B.** star (noun): a famous person or celebrity **C.** star (verb): putting a mark next to something for special notice

____ 1. Everyone began taking pictures when they saw the star in the restaurant.

____ 2. The night was so clear that the boys could see a shooting star.

____ 3. Serena starred the things she wanted the most on her birthday list.

Challenge: Choose a definition, and write a sentence using the word *stars*.

_____

_____

<u>wave</u> the white flag	**A.** wave (noun): a swell or surge of water in the ocean **B.** wave (verb): to shake or move a hand around as a friendly gesture **C.** wave (verb): to cause to bend or sway, usually by weather

____ 4. The wind caused the flag to wave in the air.

____ 5. Brandon was nervous about starting at a new school, but he was excited when another student waved at him from across the playground.

____ 6. The huge wave caused the surfers to fall off their surfboards into the cold water.

Challenge: Choose a definition, and write a sentence using the word *wave*.

_____

_____

Patriotic Days: Stars and Stripes—Wacky Writing

Directions: Read and answer each prompt.

1. Describe a time when you might want to *change your stripes*.

   _____

   _____

   _____

2. What famous figure would cause you to have *stars in your eyes*? Why?

   _____

   _____

   _____

3. Describe a time when it would be a good idea to *wave a white flag* instead of continuing to fight or disagree with someone.

   _____

   _____

   _____

4. When meeting someone for the first time, name two things that would be *red flags* for you, suggesting that he or she may not be a good person to befriend.

   _____

   _____

   _____

5. Name one goal you currently have that makes you feel that you are *aiming for the stars*. How far along are you in your goal?

   _____

   _____

   _____

Patriotic Days: Stars and Stripes—Say What? Extensions

Directions: Choose two activities to complete.

> » aim for the stars
>
> » a red flag
>
> » wave the white flag
>
> » change your stripes
>
> » stars in one's eyes

Short Story

Write a short description of something that recently happened to you using two of the figures of speech. Be sure the figures of speech are used correctly. Underline them when you are finished.

👓 Read All About It!

With a partner, pretend you work for a news organization and have to write one paragraph about something that happened in your town. The story should contain at least two of this week's figures of speech.

Actor's Studio

In a small group, brainstorm five additional figures of speech. Write this week's figures of speech and the five additional figures of speech on small slips of paper. Then, divide into two teams and play a short game of charades using the figures of speech as the secret phrases.

stars in one's eyes

Figures of Speech

» talk turkey

» thank your lucky stars

» quitting cold turkey

» feast your eyes on something

» as you sow, so shall you reap

Overview

Students will enjoy learning about Thanksgiving-related figures of speech through the activities in this section. For detailed instructions on how to implement the activities in this lesson, see pages 8–10.

Materials

> copies of *Thanksgiving—Match That Figure!* (page 127)

> copies of *Thanksgiving—Would You Rather?* (page 128)

> copies of *Thanksgiving—Meaningful Words* (page 129)

> copies of *Thanksgiving—Wacky Writing* (page 130)

> copies of *Thanksgiving—Say What? Extensions* (page 131)

> scissors and glue

> index cards

Additional Figures of Speech

> thank heavens

> no thanks to you

> meat and potatoes

> drop it like a hot potato

> how do you like them apples?

Answer Key

Match That Figure! (page 127)

1. to enjoy the sight of someone or something

2. things will happen to you according to how you behave or plan

3. to be thankful for your luck in a situation

4. quitting something quickly and abruptly

5. to talk serious business

Pictures will vary but should show an understanding for each figure of speech.

Would You Rather? (page 128)

Check sentences to be sure students' explanations answer the questions.

Meaningful Words (page 129)

1. B   2. A   3. C

Challenge: Check sentences to be sure contexts match the definitions chosen.

4. B   5. B   6. A

Challenge: Check sentences to be sure contexts match the definitions chosen.

Wacky Writing (page 130)

Students' responses should accurately answer each prompt and demonstrate understanding of the figurative phrase.

Say What? Extensions (page 131)

Check to see that students have completed two of the three activities.

Thanksgiving—Match That Figure!

Directions: Cut apart the cards below. Glue each definition next to the correct figure of speech. Then, draw a picture to represent each figurative phrase.

Figures of speech	Definitions	Pictures
1. feast your eyes on something (idiom)		
2. as you sow, so shall you reap (proverb)		
3. thank your lucky stars (idiom)		
4. quitting cold turkey (idiom)		
5. talk turkey (idiom)		

quitting something quickly and abruptly	to talk serious business	things will happen to you according to how you behave or plan	to enjoy the sight of someone or something	to be thankful for your luck in a situation

Thanksgiving—Would You Rather?

Directions: Read and answer each question.

1. Would you rather *thank your lucky stars* for a new smartphone or a new pet? Why?

   _____

   _____

   _____

2. Would you rather quit eating sweets or drinking soda *cold turkey*? Why?

   _____

   _____

   _____

3. Would you rather have a friend or a family member with you if you had to *talk turkey* in business? Why?

   _____

   _____

   _____

4. Would you rather *feast your eyes* on a sunset or a rainstorm? Why?

   _____

   _____

   _____

5. Write your own question using the phrase *as you sow, so shall you reap*.

   _____

   _____

   _____

Name _____ Date _____

Thanksgiving—Meaningful Words

Directions: For each sentence, write the letter of the correct definition. Then, create your own sentence using the selected word.

quitting <u>cold</u> turkey	**A.** cold (noun): a common illness characterized by sneezing and coughing **B.** cold (adverb): suddenly or quickly **C.** cold (adjective): not affectionate or friendly

____ 1. Bert was so tired from running the marathon that as soon as he lay down he was out cold.

____ 2. Her cold caused her to miss three days of work.

____ 3. Her cold response to his hug let him know that something was wrong.

Challenge: Choose a definition, and write a sentence using the word *cold*.

_____

_____

<u>talk</u> turkey	**A.** talk (verb): to communicate and exchange ideas by speaking **B.** talk (noun): an informal speech or lecture

____ 4. Jeb's mom had a talk with her son after he got in trouble in class.

____ 5. Professor Liu gave a pep talk to his class before they took their final exam.

____ 6. The old friends talked all night after not seeing each other for years.

Challenge: Choose a definition, and write a sentence using the word *talk*.

_____

_____

Thanksgiving—Wacky Writing

Directions: Read and answer each prompt.

1. Name a time you would prefer to *talk turkey* instead of having to beat around the bush.

   _____

   _____

   _____

2. Describe a meal you could *feast your eyes on* that would make your mouth water before you even started eating.

   _____

   _____

   _____

3. Describe a time when you could have gotten badly hurt, but you *thanked your lucky stars* nothing bad happened.

   _____

   _____

   _____

4. Do you think it is easier to quit a habit slowly over time or *quit cold turkey*? Why?

   _____

   _____

   _____

5. Describe a time that you put effort into something and earned the rewards later, proving that *as you sow, so shall you reap*.

   _____

   _____

   _____

Thanksgiving—Say What? Extensions

Directions: Choose two activities to complete.

> » talk turkey   » thank your lucky stars
>
> » quitting cold turkey   » feast your eyes on something
>
> » as you sow, so shall you reap

 ## Say It, Don't Spray It!

Work with a small group to write and tell a story that includes all five figures of speech. One person begins the story. Then, each person takes a turn adding an idea to the story. Continue the story until all figures of speech have been used and the story comes to an end.

 ## Comic Strip

Create a short four- to six-frame comic strip with sketches or simple pictures. Show the humor of one character using a figure of speech and the other character taking it literally.

 ## Memory Game

Using 10 index cards, write each figure of speech and each definition on a separate card. Then, turn them over and play a quick memory game with a partner. Play twice to see who can get the most overall matches between the games.

talk turkey

References Cited

Blachowicz, Camille, and Peter J. Fisher. 2014. *Teaching Vocabulary in All Classrooms*. 5th ed. New York, NY: Pearson.

Harris, Theodore Lester, and Richard E. Hodges. 1995. *The Literacy Dictionary: The Vocabulary of Reading and Writing*. Newark, DE: International Reading Association.

National Reading Panel. 2000. *The Report of the National Reading Panel*. Washington, DC: US Department of Education.

Additional Resources

Teachers can use the classroom resource list below to learn more about how to incorporate figurative language instruction into the classroom.

"Books with Figurative Language." *This Reading Mama*. http://thisreadingmama.com/books-figurative-language/.

Colston, Herbert L., and Melissa S. Kuiper. 2002. "Figurative Language Development Research and Popular Children's Literature: Why We Should Know 'Where the Wild Things Are.'" *Metaphor and Symbol* 17 (1): 27–43.

Hazelton, Rebecca. 2015. "Learning About Figurative Language: How to Use Simile and Metaphor Like a Boss." *Poetry Foundation*. April 13, 2015. http://www.poetryfoundation.org/learning/article/250298.

"Homepage—ReadWriteThink." *Readwritethink.org*. http://www.readwritethink.org/.

Palmer, Barbara C., Vikki S. Shackelford, and Judith T. Leclere. 2006. "Bridging Two Worlds: Reading Comprehension, Figurative Language Instruction, and the English Language Learner." *Journal of Adolescent and Adult Literacy* 50 (4): 258–267.

Petrosky, Anthony R. 1980. "The Inferences We Make: Children and Literature." *Language Arts* 57 (2): 149–156.

Rasinski, Timothy. 2008. *Idioms and Other English Expressions: 1–3*. Huntington Beach, CA: Shell Education.

Rasinski, Timothy. 2008. *Idioms and Other English Expressions: 4–6*. Huntington Beach, CA: Shell Education.

Rasinski, Timothy, and Melissa Cheesman Smith. 2014. *Vocabulary Ladders: Understanding Word Nuances*. Huntington, CA: Teacher Created Materials.

Rasinski, Timothy, and Jerry Zutell. 2010. *Essential Strategies for Word Study: Effective Methods for Improving Decoding, Spelling, and Vocabulary*. New York, NY: Scholastic.

Spears, Richard A. 2006. *A Dictionary of American Idioms*. 4th ed. New York, NY: McGraw-Hill.

"The Best Children's Books!" *The Best Children's Books!* http://thebestchildrensbooks.org/.

"The Idiom Connection." *The Idiom Connection*. http://www.idiomconnection.com/.

Vasquez, Anete. 2005. "Literary Analysis 101." *The English Journal* 94 (6): 97–100.

Zutell, Jerry. 2016. *Word Wisdom: Unlocking Vocabulary in Context*. Columbus, OH: Zaner-Bloser.

Check It Out!

Websites

Teachers can use the websites below to learn more about how to incorporate figurative language instruction into the classroom.

Figurativelanguage.net

This website offers an in-depth explanation of figurative language: alliteration, hyperbole, imagery, irony, metaphor, onomatopoeia, oxymoron, personification, and similes.

Idiomconnection.com

This idiom website contains a comprehensive list of idioms organized alphabetically and by themes, such as animal, body, color, and food. Each section concludes with a comprehensive quiz, which tests students' knowledge of the idioms in the section.

Literarydevices.net

This website contains a comprehensive list of over 100 literary devices. Each device is coupled with multiple examples and a short section that explains the function of each literary device.

Readwritethink.org

This website is devoted to English language learning and literacy. Here, educators can find classroom and after-school resources on how to teach idioms to students in grades 3–5.

Thebestchildrensbooks.org

This site, created by three teachers, has hundreds of books listed for school-aged children. Educators can find books on many of the figurative language staples, including idioms, similes, and onomatopoeia.

Thisreadingmama.com

Becky Spence, a homeschooling-blogger-mom, compiles a detailed list of books that contain and teach figurative language. Each book on her list has a detailed explanation of what type(s) of figurative language can be found in the book and some of the themes present in the book.

Children's Books with Figurative Language

The list below offers great examples of figurative language for students across all grade levels.

Arnold, Tedd. 2003. *More Parts*. New York, NY: Puffin Books.

———. 2007. *Even More Parts*. New York, NY: Puffin Books.

Brinckloe, Julie. 1986. *Fireflies!* New York, NY: Aladdin.

Burton, Virginia Lee. 1978. *The Little House*. New York, NY: HMH Books for Young Readers.

Cleary, Brian P. 2009. *Skin Like Milk, Hair of Silk: What are Similes and Metaphors?* Minneapolis, MN: Millbrook Press.

Floca, Brian. 2013. *Locomotive*. New York, NY: Atheneum Books.

Frazee, Marla. 2006. *Roller Coaster*. New York, NY: HMH Books for Young Readers.

Gobel, Paul. 1993. *The Girl Who Loved Wild Horses*. New York, NY: Aladdin.

Gwynne, Fred. 1988. *A Chocolate Moose for Dinner*. New York, NY: Aladdin.

———. 1988. *The King Who Rained*. New York, NY: Aladdin.

Leedy, Loren. 2003. *There's a Frog in My Throat: 440 Animal Sayings a Little Bird Told Me*. New York, NY: Holiday House.

———. 2009. *Crazy like a Fox: A Simile Story*. New York, NY: Holiday House.

Parish, Peggy. 1963. *Amelia Bedelia*. New York, NY: HarperCollins.

Piven, Hanoch. 2007. *My Dog is as Smelly as Dirty Socks: And Other Funny Family Portraits*. New York, NY: Schwartz and Wade.

———. 2010. *My Best Friend is as Sharp as a Pencil*. New York, NY: Random House.

———. 2013. *My Dog is as Smelly as Dirty Socks*. New York, NY: Random House.

Potter, Beatrix. 1902. *The Complete Tales of Peter the Rabbit*. New York, NY: Penguin.

Prelutsky, Jack. 1999. *20th Century Children's Poetry Treasury*. New York, NY: Knopf Books for Young Readers.

Teague, Mark. 2004. *Pigsty*. New York, NY: Scholastic.

Terban, Marvin. 1983. *In a Pickle*. New York, NY: Houghton Mifflin.

Tresselt, Alvin. 1988. *White Snow, Bright Snow*. New York, NY: HarperCollins.

Silverstein, Shel. 1964. *The Giving Tree*. New York, NY: HarperCollins.

———. 1974. *Where the Sidewalk Ends*. New York, NY: HarperCollins.

Steig, William. 1969. *Sylvester and the Magic Pebble*. New York, NY: Aladdin.

Van Allsburg, Chris. 1985. *The Polar Express*. New York, NY: HMH Books for Young Readers.

———. 1988. *Two Bad Ants*. New York, NY: HMH Books for Young Readers.

Weston, Carol. 2015. *Taco Cat*. Naperville, IL: Sourcebooks Jabberwocky.

Winter, Jeanette. 1988. *Follow the Drinking Gourd*. New York, NY: Random House.

Wood, Audrey. 1990. *Quick as a Cricket*. Auburn, ME: Child's Play International Limited.

Yolen, Jane. 1987. *Owl Moon*. New York, NY: Philomel Books.

Young, Ed. 2002. *Seven Blind Mice*. New York, NY: Puffin Books.